101 Games and Activities for Children with Autism, Asperger's, and Sensory Processing Disorders

TARA DELANEY, M.S., OTR

New York Chicago San Francisco Lisbon London Madrid Mexico City
Milan New Delhi San Juan Seoul Singapore Sydney Toronto

Library of Congress Cataloging-in-Publication Data

Delaney, Tara.
    101 games and activities for children with autism, Asperger's, and sensory
    processing disorder / Tara Delaney.
        p.   cm.
        ISBN 987-0-07-162336-0 (alk. paper)
        1. Autism in children—Patients—Rehabilitation.   2. Asperger's syndrome
    in children—Patients—Rehabilitation.   3. Sensory disorders in children—
    Patients—Rehabilitation.   4.Games   I. Title   II. Title: One hundred one
    games and activities for children with autism, Asperger's, and sensory processing
    disorder.   III. Title: One hundred and one games and activities for children with
    autism, Asperger's, and sensory processing disorder.

    RJ506.A9 D442   2010
    618.92'858832—dc22   2009009924

*To the Currys, Goukers, and Crevers for teaching
me how much love and persistence can
change a child's life. Thank you.*

19 20 21 22   QVS   21 20 19

ISBN 978-0-07-162336-0
MHID   0-07-162336-1

Interior design by Monica Baziuk

McGraw-Hill books are available at special quantity discounts to use as premiums and
sales promotions, or for use in corporate training programs. To contact a representative
please e-mail us at bulksales@mcgraw-hill.com.

This book is printed on acid-free paper.

CONTENTS

ACKNOWLEDGMENTS

J OHN, MY EDITOR at McGraw-Hill, for implicitly understanding that we can teach more through play than any other way. Your passion has energized this project.

I owe a deep thanks to June Clark of Fine Print Literary Agency for her extraordinary ability to connect people and ideas. I will always be grateful for your friendship and professional insight.

I am incredibly grateful and humbled by the team at Steps Therapy, Inc. Your expertise and drive are only surpassed by your passion to truly make a difference in the lives of the children we serve. A special thanks goes to those therapists who assisted with editing and suggestions. Your input was invaluable. To Mary Hamrick, director of Speech Therapy and cocreator of the Social Sense™ program. Thank you for hearing me out on all my ideas, embracing those that make sense, shaking your head at those that do not, and always listening.

To the educators, therapists, and administrators in the following school districts: Lago Vista, Texas; Marble Falls, Texas; Nevada

County (California) Office of Education; Rocklin, California; Wheatland, California; Woodland, California; and Yuba County (California) Office of Education for your continuous commitment to improving the education of children through conventional and creative avenues. My sincere appreciation goes to Elaine Leeds, Pat Muniz, Melissa Orcutt, and Kristen Nottle-Powell. I have learned so much by being part of the team for so many years.

Barbara McPhillips, principal at The New York Institute of Special Education, your belief in the value of each child's life serves as an example to us all.

A huge thanks to Dr. Lucy Jane Miller and the SPD Foundation for the diligence to expand research into sensory processing disorder as well as autism.

To my dad for saying, "You should do that, Tara" when his six-year-old daughter said, "Someday I'm going help kids" and for never questioning dreams only challenging them to come true. To my mom who thinks I know more than I really do. Thanks for setting the bar high, I'll keep jumping.

To Maggie and Liam, my precious babies, who teach me things everyday through play. To my husband, Bill, whose intellect and passion keep making my dreams come true. Thank you for showing me that life is best lived believing you can.

INTRODUCTION

I WAS FIVE, almost six years old, when I first understood the power of play. My mother had just passed away, and I felt lost. My father found an older couple to babysit my sister and me after school so he could work. One of the other children they babysat was a little girl about my age. She had developmental disabilities and did not speak very much. She was standing and waiting in the driveway almost every day when the school bus dropped me off at the babysitter's house. I remember not knowing what to say to her or even how to act, but looking forward to seeing her there waiting.

One day when I got off the bus, she was holding a ball. She threw the ball toward me, and it dropped to the ground. I did not know what to say to her, but I knew what to do with a ball. I put my books on the grass, picked up the ball, and threw it back to her. She laughed and then moved her arms forward to try to catch it. The ball landed on the grass again. She picked it up and threw it back at me. I caught the ball and returned her laugh. Her willingness to engage me in a game of catch started a connection that was a childhood lifeline for me.

Many years later when I became an occupational therapist, I thought of Sheila and how powerful the act of participating in a simple game of catch was to my life. It wasn't until I began my career that I could reflect on how powerful it was to *her* life also.

In my early career, I returned to graduate school at the University of Wisconsin where I participated in a leadership training program at the Waisman Center in Madison. As part of that program, I was assigned to a family who had a little boy with neurological difficulties. I was assigned to the family not as a therapist but rather as another family member. I ate dinner with them from time to time, went to the park with them, was there at bedtime, and even babysat on some occasions. By being with this little boy and his family during everyday activities, I could see how sensory processing and communication difficulties impacted his daily life and how things that were enticing and fun for other children were a reason for fear and avoidance to him. But I also saw firsthand how his parents used sensory strategies, in the form of play, to help him engage with the people in his life. With both of these memories, the big "Aha" for me is the power that play has to teach, develop, and connect children to their world.

I cannot say enough about interactive, physical play as a basis for teaching children skills that are fundamental to their physical and social world and to their cognitive capabilities. The dynamic nature of play spurs nervous system development by connecting the brain and the body. In addition to my own experience, research has shown that there is no substitute for play for promoting learning at the nervous system level, as well as for teaching more refined language, social, and cognitive concepts. During play, children are provided the opportunity to use their bodies to manipulate objects in their physical world, which is the only way to truly understand the physical and spatial properties of their world. Because of play's interactive nature, it sets the perfect stage for teaching language concepts and reinforcing an intuitive understanding of others.

As a pediatric occupational therapist, I have spent the last two decades working with children who have neurological difficulties. When working with these children, the primary goal of my therapy is the acquisition of new skills (sensory, motor, social, and academic). I realized many years ago that a child's motivation to participate in an activity is one of the most important factors in determining successful engagement. Successful engagement is the first step to learning. It is with this idea in mind that I created games or adapted activities that focus on particular skills *and* are highly enjoyable to children. I have been compiling dozens of games and activities over the years, many of which are in this book.

The activities and games in this book are organized to reflect a model of child development called the Brain Library™. I developed this model as a way to explain to parents and educators how important our early experiences are for future academic and social success. The experiences that we engage in during our early years of life introduce, develop, and refine skills that our brains and bodies will need to access throughout our lives. Books are metaphors for experiences. Each of our experiences, beginning in utero, in a sense writes books into our Brain Library.

In the early years, the majority of our experiences are sensorimotor. These experiences write books that build the foundation of our Brain Library. The books of the Brain Library are organized into three main sections: the foundation section, the integrated skills section, and the capabilities section. The *foundation section* houses our basic senses: vestibular (balance and motion), proprioceptive (body position), tactile (touch), visual (seeing), auditory (hearing), gustatory (taste), and olfactory (smell). The *integrated*

The Brain Library™

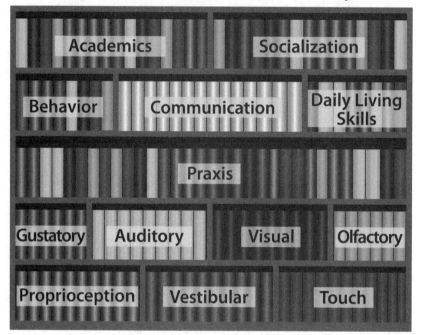

skills section contains the skills that allow us to interact and thrive as human beings: praxis (ability to plan movement), which takes up an entire shelf; daily living skills; behavior; and communication. The *capabilities category* includes the key factors to success in our modern world: social intelligence and cognitive intelligence. Please note that you'll find more detailed definitions of these and other terms in the glossary at the end of the book.

Your child's brain is in a constant state of gathering, storing, and retrieving information while he is developing. The stored books are used as references to give a context for when your child is presented with a new activity, as well as to provide a framework for how to navigate the current situation. This process of gathering, categorizing, and storing new information in the Brain Library for later referencing is the basis for learning.

As you go through the activities in this book, keep in mind that they are designed to accomplish three goals simultaneously: first is to reference and develop sensory systems, second is to introduce learning concepts, and third is to infuse language into all aspects of your child's life. Many children with neurological difficulties such as autism spectrum disorder (ASD), Asperger's syndrome, and sensory processing disorder process information in a way that impedes them from readily seeking out experiences that lead to exploration about themselves and the physical environment surrounding them. It is my belief that as parents, educators, and therapists, we must set up the physical world (activities) in such a way as to entice engagement and experiences that will write and store books in children's Brain Libraries for their future success.

101 Games and Activities for Children with Autism, Asperger's, and Sensory Processing Disorders includes games and activities that incorporate strategies proven to be effective in helping children apply meaning to novel and play situations. By giving children tools to participate *and* "have fun" in a new game or activity, you are laying the groundwork to increase their engagement in the world around them.

Children with neurological difficulties often do not track to the established developmental-age charts. When deciding which activities will best promote your child's development, it is important to remember that your child's skill level may be different from his or her chronological age. With that said, keep two very important things in mind when playing with your child. First, patience is more than a virtue—it is a necessity. Second, if your child is having difficulty understanding the game or has sensory fears that are preventing him or her from completely engaging, it is important to adapt the game so that you alleviate fears and increase engagement. For example, if the game requires a swing and your child is afraid, lower the swing a bit so she can keep her feet on the ground and rock back and forth. It is important to remember that your child may not understand all the components of an activity but may be successful in one component of the activity. Capitalize on that, keep reinforcing the other parts of the activity, and it will gradually increase your child's understanding of the entire activity.

Today, he'll stack one block upon another—eyes, fingers, nerves, and muscles working together—never realizing that with this simple task, he's laying the foundation for all those tomorrows when he'll spell his name, compose his first story, write his first love letter, and, before you know it, pen a bestselling novel and then, of course, win the Nobel Prize.
—Pediatric Occupational Therapy Association

THE *HOW* OF ENGAGEMENT

I T IS OFTEN said that play is work for children with neurological difficulties, especially autism, Asperger's syndrome, and sensory processing disorder. This is understandable since many children with a neurological challenges struggle with expressive and receptive language skills, motor planning, as well as sensory processing. These struggles ultimately impact the ability of these children to initiate and engage in free play. The challenge is compounded because they have difficulty learning by watching others—another key element of play. Also, social interaction, in and of itself, is not highly motivating for many of these children, especially children with autism or Asperger's, so they are not naturally inclined to seek out other children to play with. However, reports from parents, educators, and therapists, as well as my own experience show that when these children are taught effective ways to engage with objects and people to expand their sensory, motor, language, and social skills, they have fun!

ASSUME A CONNECTION

Increasing a child's engagement in the world around him or her is the main objective of the games and activities in this book. Getting and holding the interest of some children may seem futile at times. The challenge when playing with and teaching children with neurological difficulties is that we, caretakers and educators, judge a child's interest based on the feedback he or she gives us. However, children with autism, Asperger's, or sensory processing disorder may not give typical feedback, even as infants. We may find ourselves decreasing or changing our engagement level, ultimately giving the child less input or fewer experiences. Often our motivation is to protect our children or simply not to overstimulate them, but instead we limit their opportunities to learn how to connect.

As a therapist, I see that children with neurological difficulties are exposed to fewer sensorimotor and language experiences compared to typically developing children, often because these children don't give feedback that shows they are interested in playing or being spoken to. Some may even give negative feedback to parenting input, such as arching away when we hold them, averting eye contact, not watching the caretaker with their eyes, as well as having adverse reactions to certain sensory stimulation, such as movement or touch. When a young child doesn't appear to register what we say or do, or appears to register it in a negative or fearful way, the natural reaction is to pull back and give less. We may not even realize we are doing this. It is simply a natural response that occurs during all human interactions.

When we smile at or talk to babies, they smile back or even laugh and coo; then we smile and coo back, responding to the baby's positive feedback. When that doesn't happen, we start doing it less because we are not getting the expected feedback. Interaction is reciprocal, so when someone talks less to us, we also tend to talk to that person less. When parents put their child on a swing at the playground and the child screams, most parents take the child off the swing—and it may be a while before the parents try to put the child back on the swing. If the parent gets the same reaction on the next attempt, that parent may never try the swing again. The same applies for other experiences, such as touching certain textures, listening to certain types of music, or eating different types of foods that your child may react to negatively. Soon the lack of response or the negative response changes our behavior as adults because we intuitively pull back on input that is not garnering positive responses from the child. In essence, we as caretakers become trained by the child to verbally interact less or even guard the child from sensorimotor input the child has reacted to adversely.

When we interact with any children, including children with neurological difficulties, we have to assume that they are connecting to us and that they are getting something from the interaction *even if it doesn't seem as if they are*. We cannot judge their level of interest strictly by the feedback they give; otherwise we are prone to give less. We need to be careful not to allow ourselves to give less, as these children need more, not less, input. As you participate with your child in the activities in this book, assume that the child's nervous system is enriched by the experience. Assume that you are connecting to your child and he or she is connecting to you, even if it doesn't seem like it. Remember, for children with neurological difficulties to store and access information, they need higher levels of input infused in many different ways. The key is ever-increasing engagement of your child.

Baby Steps

If an activity is perceived as too complicated or too long, many children will not engage. To be motivated, they need to perceive activities as being "fun" because the children who don't have a clear picture of where to begin and where the activity is heading will be reluctant to participate. This is true for neurologically typical children as well as for children with neurological difficulties. Therefore, one of the keys when teaching a child a new game or activity is to break the activity into smaller parts and demonstrate one part of the activity exclusive to the other parts. Once a child understands and has mastered one part, you can start adding more parts to the activity. You are stringing together mastered tasks that if done sequentially complete a whole activity or game. Keep this in mind as you go through the games and exercises in this book; if your child has difficulty understanding the entire "game," try breaking it down into smaller, more manageable tasks.

Motor Learning

While you are watching another person perform a physical activity, motor neurons in the brain called *mirror neurons* fire as if you were performing the activity yourself. For example, when you watch somebody throw a baseball, the same motor neurons that fire in that person's body when throwing the ball fire in your body when you watch him. Studies have shown that individuals with autism do not have the same mirror neuron responses as people who are considered neurotypical. Since many children with neurological difficulties have a difficult time processing movement information or replicating motor actions, having them watch somebody do something may not be enough—you may have to physically guide your child through a new motor action several times before his or her body "gets it."

If your child appears not to know how to make his or her body do what you are asking, then your child's brain may not be able to learn motor tasks by observation only. Physically teach your child by moving his or her body through the new activity while verbally saying what the child's body is doing. For example, if you are showing a child how to pull himself across the floor on a scooter board, move his arms in an alternating pattern in front of him so his body can feel the motor movement. Coach him the entire time, telling him to pull with his right arm and then with his left arm. Once the child's body understands how to move to accomplish the action, the child will be able to perform the action independently.

REINFORCERS

Some children are motivated to engage in a new activity simply because it is novel, while other children will shy away from anything new, or even familiar, unless a tangible reinforcer is present. Simply said, some activities are internally motivating (naturally reinforced) for some children, while other activities will require external reinforcers to motivate a child to attempt or engage in the activity. This does not mean that the activity is not fun for the child. It simply means that your child has difficulty *perceiving* the activity as fun or something the child is capable of doing. Once the child is engaged or has some mastery over the activity, the child's understanding of the activity increases, as does the child's enjoyment. So the cycle begins: with increased enjoyment comes increased engagement, which begets increased enjoyment.

A reinforcer can be tangible such as a food item or a sensory toy, or it can even be embedded in the activity or game. For example, if the game involves a scooter board, the reinforcement might be getting to crash the scooter board into a large pillow. Since many children with neurological difficulties have fear reactions to certain stimuli, it is important to understand this and pair possibly frightening new stimuli with external reinforcers that you know the child likes.

Social reinforcement is the obvious display of pleasure from another because of our actions or words. It ranges from a big bear hug or clapping to a wink or simple acceptance into a group. Social reinforcement is one of the fundamental drivers of human behavior. As parents we want our children to be motivated by the positive reinforcement of ourselves and others. So every time they complete a portion of the activity, smile and cheer for them. It is important to remember many children on the spectrum do not appear to be motivated by social reinforcers, and that is why using tangible reinforcers along with the normal social reinforcement may be required. By linking a social reinforcer with a tangible reinforcer, you are helping the child understand that the social component is positive, and the child will start to seek the social reinforcer because he or she will understand it as a reward.

When using reinforcers, it is important to understand certain things about behavior related to reinforcers. First, if anyone is exposed to the same reinforcer over and over again, that person eventually reaches a saturation point known as *satiation*. Exposure to a certain reinforcer over and over again results in decrease in interest of the item. For example, if you love chocolate and someone gave you a chocolate bar every hour, you would relish it. But after several bars, you would not be motivated by the chocolate any longer, because you would have reached a satiation point. The same thing happens to children when you give them the same thing over and over—the encouragement or external reward you give them loses its effectiveness. The way around this is to offer different reinforcers or random reinforcers.

Differentiating reinforcers can be very effective when teaching a complex activity because you use reinforcers that are considered "pretty good" or "fairly desirable" for parts of the activity and you offer the "most desirable" reinforcer when the child completes the whole activity. Note that social reinforcement can also be differentiated. For example, smile and say, "That was a good *something*," when the child gets part of the activity, and then say, "Wow, amazing!" and jump up and down when the child completes the whole activity. Let the child know that different tasks or efforts result in different rewards. It is difficult for a child to judge *good*, *better*, and *best* when we give the same reinforcer each time.

Keeping several things in mind when using reinforcers will help increase the success of engagement. First, make sure the reinforcer you are using is something that your child really wants—whether it be a small, sweet treat; a particular toy; or a tickling. Also, remember that what a child likes changes continuously. Something that was reinforcing last week may be boring or even undesirable next week. Finally, the reinforcers should be offered only after the child follows through with the desired action or behavior. For example, if you are trying to teach a child to "wait" between her turn and yours and she does, reward her instantly. If she doesn't, make sure not to give her the reward, or you diminish the power of using reinforcers.

When you use *outside* reinforcers, meaning reinforcers that are not part of the activity or game, make sure you label the behavior you are rewarding. Say, "That was good waiting," as you give the child a big hug or a small piece of cookie. Using a particular character who already is a strong fixture in your child's life, such as Thomas the Tank Engine, Lightning McQueen, or Dora, to motivate the child to do something is simultaneously reinforcing and motivating for your child. For example, my four-year-old son does not readily switch from one activity to the next. So if he is in the midst of playing, the idea of leaving and going to the store is not acceptable. However, if Thomas is going along to be Mommy's helper by watching where Mommy drives and finding apples at the store for Mommy, my son will go because Thomas is going!

As your child learns the basics of participating in an activity or game such as waiting, following directions, and requesting help, you will be able to move away from the more tangible reinforcers and move toward more natural reinforcers. Natural reinforcers are considered internally driven reinforcers, such as the good feeling that comes from success at an activity or in a social situation. When you see that a child is becoming internally motivated by the activity itself, start to gradually decrease the tangible reinforcers and opt for the more natural reinforcers.

Visual Cues

One of the most powerful tools to use when teaching anything, new or familiar, with all children is a visual schedule. It has been well documented that children on the spectrum rely heavily on their visual systems to understand their environment. Visual cues are powerful tools to aid any child and increase the understanding of what to expect from a situation or "what is expected" of him or her. The use of pictures makes instructions clear and decreases frustration for both the child and the person giving instruction.

Visual cues offer more permanent information for children than does telling the child what he or she is expected to do. Although the use of visuals is promoted for teaching children with autism, I find that they are effective teaching tools for all children—especially those with neurological difficulties, such as sensory processing disorder, Asperger's syndrome, or attention deficit/hyperactivity disorder (ADHD).

When verbal or physical directions are accompanied by visuals, a child has something to refer to if he or she is not able to retain the auditory information. Pictures can be used to show the sequence of an activity or even the rules of a game. For example, you can have a child hold a picture of another child sitting to indicate waiting. The visual doesn't necessarily need to be a picture; it can be something like a medallion that is passed between two children to indicate whose turn it is to "jump into the mound of pillows."

A visual strategy that Hilary Baldi, a play-based behaviorist, employs when teaching games involving peers is a long necklace (Mardi Gras style) with a small card hanging at the end that says, "My turn." Children put it on when it is their turn; then they take it off and offer the next child the "My turn" necklace for their turn. This is an effective way to teach children how to take turns because they have to wait to exchange the necklace and the necklace physically reminds the waiting children that it is someone else's turn.

Besides using pictures or schematic drawings of directions, another excellent visual cue to help children understand the time component of an activity is the use of a timer. The Time Timer is especially effective. This visual timer shows the time remaining in red, with the red decreasing with the passage of time. Using the Time Timer in combination with a picture that shows what is happening during the time helps decrease anxiety.

SOCIAL STORY

An expanded and personalized version of visual cueing is the social story. This involves stringing together pictures and simple words to tell a story of something that has happened or will happen. It provides a way to give the child visual cues along with words to guide the child through a particular scenario and his or her role in the story. In addition, it gives the child a framework of how to act in a given situation. When peers are introduced into the activities and games, a social story detailing how to "play" a particular game with a peer and some possible scenarios of interaction may be helpful. This prepares your child ahead of time and increases his or her chance of success with peers in game situations.

Social stories are a tool used to explain potential situations, new places, or new people to children who have difficulty projecting themselves into novel situations and therefore have difficulty knowing how to act in such situations. Usually, social stories are a set of pictures accompanied by short and concise sentences, creating a book that provides children with a framework of what to expect and how to act in a given situation. You can purchase prepared social stories and even social sensory stories. However, many parents and educators become masters at creating personalized social stories. I find that the social stories that include pictures of the child are the most effective for young or nonverbal children.

INFUSING LANGUAGE

You will find that the games and activities in this book are what I call *language-rich activities.* In my experience working with children and cotreating with speech pathologists, the best way for a child to learn language is in the midst of activity. Research shows that in early life more than 90 percent of verbs are learned while the action is taking place.

When children learn while engaging in the action, they are more likely to have developed motor memory of the action linked to the verb. For example, they will understand the word *jump* better if they are jumping while they learn it. Furthermore, the best way to learn descriptors for the physical qualities of objects is by interacting with those objects: having the child hold a pillow while you are teaching the word *soft*, for example, is the best way to go. Additionally, spatial concepts are best understood in a three-dimensional world (*big, small, on top of*, etc.); children learn these kinds of words best when they are appropriately interacting with the words.

Helping Them to Use Language

You can use several strategies in the midst of fun games and activities to help elicit increased verbal responses from your child.

- Engage with your child by first blowing bubbles or winding a toy and then just stopping and waiting for your child to ask for help or say, "Go again" or "More."
- Always respond immediately to verbal output.
- Once you have played a familiar game with a child several times, you can begin setting up the game. Leave off some parts, such as the hammers for Whac-A-Mole or the shapes for Candy Land Castle, and then wait for the child to request the desired parts.
- Put things together for a game the wrong way, and wait for your child to correct you (do this only once a child has a clear understanding of how it should be put together).
- Use music and movement to increased language output. For example, sing "Row, Row, Row, Your Boat" several times while pushing a child on a swing; then leave off part of the song and wait for the child to chime in.
- While pushing a child, stop the swing, hold, and prompt the child to say, "Go," "Push," or "Again" before pushing the child again.

Always talk, talk, and talk some more when playing with your child. The key for children with neurological difficulties is to keep the language clear and concise and, when necessary, to link words to pictures. Make sure that what you are saying is related to the activity that is taking place, which means you have to stay on task, too. If you are playing with a child and talking to someone else about something completely unrelated, the child may become very confused. Always interject as much purposeful language as possible!

The main purpose of many of the activities and games in this book is to teach certain language concepts. To increase a child's language acquisition, as well as enrich the child's vocabulary, remember to keep the language simple and concise when giving directions or the child may become confused.

SENSORY SENSITIVITIES

Sensory sensitivities can impede a child's participation in activities that would otherwise be considered fun or enticing for most children. Many of these activities are designed to increase sensory exposure in a fun, safe way that will help children with sensory disorders become more comfortable with uncomfortable sensations. When playing with your child who is sensory-sensitive, try to start with the activities that use deep-pressure input along with exposure to tactile or movement input. Deep-pressure input has a calming effect on the nervous system, counteracting the reactions to sensory input that would otherwise be perceived as noxious. As adults we can relate to the calming effects of deep-pressure input when we've been on the receiving end of a firm hug or deep-tissue massage.

If you see that your child is beginning to pull back from a particular sensory stimuli that is a normal part of a given activity, alter the activity or move on to another one. Many of the activities and games in this book offer differing levels as well as ways to do them with different materials. Also, using visual cues for children who have sensory processing difficulties (which is most children with neurological difficulties) helps decrease anxiety, since they know what to expect. If they can see what is coming next, it will help them become more comfortable with the activity.

If your sensory-sensitive child is nonverbal, pay increased attention to any physiological reactions to input such as sweating, darting eyes, heavy breathing, and agitated movement. These are signs that your child is having a fright reaction (sometimes referred to as fight or flight) to the sensory input or his perception of the input. The term *fight or flight* is what is in the literature; however, my interpretation after years of working with children is that the physiological response is fright that then may result in fight-, flight-, or fort-type behaviors, such as being physically aggressive toward those around them, running away from a situation, simply fixating the eyes in an attempt to block out the stimuli, or forting themselves from the outside world. For children who tend to be quick to a fright reaction, it is crucial to pay close attention to the extraneous sensory environment and to prepare them for upcoming events or new people they may encounter.

INTEGRATING PEERS

Once your child has been exposed to different types of play, such as sensory or motor activities, and has developed an understanding of simple rules for traditional games, integrating peers into the play situations is the next step and is key to helping your child expand his capabilities.

By teaching your child specific skills that are essential for play, such as reciprocating the actions of another, maintaining attention on an activity, as well as engaging in representational use of objects, you supply the child with the tools of peer play. This gives the child an inroad to being a part of their peers' social world. As your child begins to successfully interact with peers in play, your child will be able to learn from his or her peers in turn, requiring less adult direction. Learning from peers has been widely encouraged by many professionals working with children with autism, Asperger's, as well as sensory processing disorder because this peer learning usually occurs in numerous settings, is dynamic, and lends to increased generalization to other people and environments.

When introducing peers into new games or activities, start with small amounts of time and familiar activities. Many of the activities in this book expand familiar activities to incorporate peers into them. When your child is first learning to play with peers, do not expect the entire play time to be filled with free, undirected play. Chances are your child will do little to no interacting with the peer or will attempt interaction but not understand how to follow through.

To better set it up, determine a short amount of time for a play date (one hour or less when you are first introducing your child to play dates), and then set up specific activities or games. I suggest alternating between fine motor or tabletop games and gross motor games that require less interaction. If two children are simply jumping on a trampoline with the objective of getting all the bears to jump off together as they laugh their heads off, they have begun the process of building a relationship, even if they are not directly interacting with one another. Some of the best friendships begin with a shared laugh!

2

SENSORY DEVELOPMENT

A WELL-DEVELOPED SENSORY system is essential for both cognitive and social intelligence, which are generally the main determinants for success in our world. Sensory development begins in utero and lays the foundation for the development of our more integrated skills, such as gross and fine motor coordination as well as language and communication.

As mentioned in the Introduction, the first two shelves of your child's Brain Library are dedicated to the basic sensory systems. Books are a metaphor for experiences. Each experience you engage in simultaneously references, writes, and stores books in your Brain Library. The books associated with your senses comprise the foundation section of your brain's library. Seven senses comprise your sensory system:

- **Vestibular (movement-balance):** This is the king of all of the senses and the most powerful system. It is also the one people are least aware of. The vestibular sense is your three-dimensional "you are here" marker, allowing you to understand where your body is in relation to the ground. The receptors for this sense are located in the vestibule in the inner ear; it indicates where you are relative to the ground and other objects.

- **Proprioceptive (body position):** This is your body awareness system. It is the "left hand knows what your right hand is doing" sense. It tells you where all of your body parts are relative to the others and how they are moving in relation to each other. Proprioceptive processing difficulties are usually linked with tactile or vestibular processing difficulties. Note: deep-pressure input, which stimulates the proprioceptive receptors, has a calming impact on the nervous system.

- **Tactile (touch):** This is your touching sense. It tells you what is in contact with your body and gives you information related to pain, pressure, temperature, movement, size, texture, and shape. Your touch sense is divided into two categories, your defensive system and your discriminative system. The defensive system is your protective touch system that alerts you to potentially harmful stimuli, such as a mosquito landing on your arm or the faint touch of a stranger behind you. The discriminative system is the part of your touch sense that gives you information about the physical nature of the objects you are touching or those that are touching you, where on the body you are being touched, temperature, as well as the pressure of what is touching you.

- **Auditory (hearing):** This is your hearing sense. It allows you to locate, capture, and discriminate sounds. The receptors for the auditory system are located in your inner ear and share some of the nerve fibers with the vestibular system. Auditory sensitivities (termed *auditory defensiveness*) are among the early concerns reported by parents of children who receive a neurological diagnosis, such as autism, Asperger's, or sensory processing disorder.

- **Visual (seeing):** This is your seeing sense. It provides you with information about color, shape, distance of objects from one another, as well as movement of objects and people. The small muscles of your eyes are controlled by your vestibular system.

- **Gustatory (taste):** This is your tasting sense; it is one of two "chemical" senses. By detecting the chemicals of foods, it gives you information about the things that enter your mouth. Coincidentally, natural chemicals that taste good are pertinent for survival.

- **Olfactory (smell):** This is your smelling sense, the other of the two "chemical" senses. By sensing chemicals in the air, it registers and categorizes information about the odors you encounter. As with food, natural chemicals that smell good often indicate safety. The part of your brain dedicated to analyzing this information has a direct neural link to the limbic system (emotional center of the brain). Many people with autism report smell sensitivities.

All of these senses depend on each other and are integrated with the other. As such difficulties in one system are likely to impact another system. For example, if your child has difficulty processing movement, he may also have difficulties processing visual input that will impact him when he is in school and needs to copy from a board or read from a book. Difficulties in these systems can also impact a child socially, because where and how a person's body relates and interacts to its surroundings is the kind of information he or she will likely need to feel secure in new environments and around new people. If your child is sensitive to touch, he will likely experience difficulties with fine motor skills that are related to academics and self-care skills.

The games and activities in this chapter are geared toward challenging and integrating the sensory systems that comprise the first two shelves of your child's Brain Library. Many of the activities require integration of information from two or more senses. The purpose is to help your child experience his sensory world in a fun way while preparing your child for more integrated skills.

GAME (1) Bonding Rock

Indoor/Outdoor

- Indoor

Equipment

- None

How

- You and another adult lock arms to create a hammock and hold the child between them in a horizontal position. Be sure both of you are close enough to apply a small amount of pressure to the child with your bodies.
- You both rock back and forth: first so the child's head is higher than the feet, then back so the feet are higher than the head.

- The entire time you are rocking sing, "Mommy, Daddy, Emma, Mommy, Daddy. . . ."
- The key is to maintain constant deep pressure on the child's body while maintaining eye contact with the child.

Purpose

- **Proprioceptive input:** The two adult bodies provide deep proprioceptive input, which is calming in much the same way swaddling a baby provides comfort.
- **Vestibular input:** The rocking back and forth provides controlled vestibular input.
- **Joint attention:** This basic activity encourages early eye contact while jointly taking part in an activity with another person.

> **WHY** Before bonding is cognitive, it is sensory. It is about the touch, auditory input, visual input, and movement shared between two people. By tying vestibular input and proprioception together and adding auditory input, you use the two most powerful sensory systems in a modified rocking activity that increases bonding between the adults and the child.

When our daughter came home from China, she was fourteen months old. She displayed some sensory defensive behaviors, including not wanting us to console her. Many times children who have not had the opportunity to physically bond with an adult caregiver become self-reliant, so much so that it impacts their ability to bond with a caretaker.

We infused many sensory activities into Maggie's life, but this game was one of the most fundamental activities that we did every day. At first, she resisted this activity. However, within several days she started to love it. As of the writing of this book she is six years old and still, every couple of months when she feels nervous or tired, she will say, "Mommy, it's time to rock Baby Maggie." My husband and I know exactly what she means.

GAME ② Feely Bag Game

Indoor/Outdoor
- Either

Equipment (First Level)
- Pillowcase
- Two identical small stuffed animals
- Two identical small balls
- Two each of common items (e.g., utensils). Be sure to use objects familiar to your child so she will not find them too difficult to identify by touch.

Equipment (Second Level)
- Paper bag (lunch size)
- Small items, such as coins, paper clips, buttons, and so on

How (First Level)
- Put one item in a pillowcase.
- Place the other identical item on a table for a visual cue.
- Have your child put his hand inside the pillowcase without looking into it. Have your child describe the item that he is feeling while he is looking at the identical item on the table. Once he

understands that the touch information matches the visual information in front of him, you can make the game more difficult.

- Increase difficulty by placing even more items on the table while the child tries to identify the item contained in the bag without looking in the bag.
- Once the child identifies the object, use expressive language to describe both action and object, such as, "You chose the penny, which is round, smooth, and flat," so that verbal communication is reinforced. Once your child begins to match descriptive language with the items, prompt him by giving him a choice of descriptors. Say things such as, "Is it soft or is it hard?" or "Is it smooth or furry?"

How (Second Level)

- Place smaller objects (one at a time) in a lunch-sized paper bag.
- Have the child identify the objects without looking (attempt to do this without visual cues).
- With increasing skill level, have the child describe, rather than just name, the object in the bag.

Purpose

- **Linking tactile input to visual input:** At the lower levels of the activity, you are teaching children to link touch information to visual information. By allowing them to view an item while they touch another identical item, you teach them to match visual properties to the descriptive touch properties. This helps them to understand the touch properties by simply viewing objects in their environment.
- **Tactile discrimination:** Using hands and fingers to determine what is in the bag without the aid of visual assistance challenges the tactile system, which lays the groundwork for fine motor skills.

- **Linking touch to language:** This game helps build a descriptive vocabulary. It is a great game for facilitating language because it builds a descriptive vocabulary.
- **Tactile sensitivities:** Since this game introduces new textures in a nonthreatening, fun way, it can be used to systematically decrease your child's sensitivities to varying textures.

Note: This is one of those "Aha"-type activities. When a child begins to identify objects and properties of objects through touch, her eyes will light up almost with a look of surprise. I love seeing children after they have played this game a few times: they put their hand in the bag, and it all clicks as they point to the matching picture or yell out, "I know . . . it's a penny!"

> **WHY** Early touch is essential for cognitive and language development. Many children with a neurological diagnosis are sensitive to touch. This hinders early learning since much of what a child learns in the early years about his or her environment is through touch. Early touch experiences also help develop fine motor skills, so it is imperative that we create fun ways to challenge and develop the tactile sense.

GAME ③ Hot Dog in a Blanket

Indoor/Outdoor

- Indoor

Equipment

- Heavy blanket
- Mommy or Daddy muscles

How

- First, lay a heavy blanket on the floor and tell your child that you're going to make "hot dogs" and your child is the hot dog. Then have your child lay at one end of the blanket (on the floor), making sure that the child's head is off the blanket before you start rolling her in the blanket. (Caution: no part of the face should be rolled in the blanket.)
- Roll the blanket and child until the blanket is wrapped around the child. Say things like, "Who's the hot dog in the bun?" Then say the child's name, "Megan is the hot dog in the bun."
- Next, apply deep pressure down the child's back (almost massagelike) while saying, "I'm putting ketchup on the hot dog's back . . . now some mustard on her arm."
- Continue applying deep pressure to arms, back, and legs in a massagelike manner. Always verbally state what body part is receiving the pressure.
- Gently pull one end of the blanket so the child rolls out of the blanket, which will make her laugh.

If your child becomes anxious being rolled up, have her put her arms outside of the blanket. This will help decrease any feelings of being contained.

Purpose

- **Proprioceptive input:** Wrapping the child in a blanket and applying the "condiments" provide deep pressure that stimulates proprioceptive receptors, thus having a calming effect on the nervous system.

■ **Communication:** While physically interacting with your child, you are also helping her identify body parts.

■ **Body awareness:** Applying deep pressure while describing the body part that you are putting the "condiment" on helps children understand how their body is connected to itself.

■ **Vestibular input:** While unrolling your child at the end of the game, you are eliciting rotary motion of the head and body, which excites the vestibular system.

■ **Learning readiness:** Rotary input is alerting to the nervous system and can be overwhelming to children who are sensitive to movement. But in this activity, rotary input is linked to proprioceptive input, which is calming to the nervous system. Stimulating the two systems together helps the nervous system achieve an optimal state of "calm alertness," making this activity an excellent warm-up to concentrated cognitive work.

Note: This game is one of my sure-to-engage standbys that I use over and over again to establish a rapport with kids while also getting them to the calm-alert stage so that they can engage in other cognitive activities.

WHY Creating activities that involve deep pressure along with vestibular-stimulating movement (rolling out of the blanket) helps the nervous system integrate itself. It also decreases a child's fear reactions to new movement, because the proprioceptive input has a calming impact on the nervous system. Thus, linking these inputs together is an effective way to increase a child's tolerance to varying movement. This is a precursor for more complex motor activities (such as sports) and cognitive activities.

GAME ④ Tic-Tac-Toe in Shaving Cream

Indoor/Outdoor

- Either

Equipment

- Shaving cream or pudding
- Flat surface (mirror is great)

How

- On a flat surface cover an area of approximately 6 inches by 6 inches with shaving cream about ½-inch thick.
- Have the child draw the four lines (two vertical, two horizontal) to create the tic-tac-toe grid in the shaving cream.
- Play tic-tac-toe in the shaving cream. At first, you can practice just making O's and X's in the boxes.
- An added fun option: use food coloring to color the shaving cream (pudding is also an option). You can also make all the X's red and all the O's blue for who's who in the game.

Purpose

- **Tactile input:** Shaving cream provides a tactile environment to practice fine motor skills.
- **Finger isolation:** This activity requires the child to use the whole hand to establish the shaving cream surface, but then the child needs to use the pointer finger in isolation to make the X's and O's.
- **Visual-motor directionality:** Creating the different directional strokes that are required for this game—for example, setting up the grid—is a precursor to letter formation.

- **Visual perceptual:** Keeping track of where the *X*'s and *O*'s are relative to the boxes of the grid and the other *X*'s and *O*'s requires visual-perceptual understanding of foreground, background, and borders.
- **Praxis and cognition:** This involves planning and organization, as well as strategy, of where to place the *X*'s and *O*'s.

WHY This activity introduces tactile input while working on basic visual-perceptual and visual-motor skills in a three-dimensional way.

GAME (5) Bubble Fun

Indoor/Outdoor

- Outdoor, preferably

Equipment

- Bottle of "blowing bubbles," including bubble-blowing wand

How

- Take turns blowing bubbles. One person pops while the other blows. Catch the bubbles on the wand and pop them on body parts.
- Alternative: Catch a bubble on the wand and then hold it away from the child and have the child blow the bubble off the wand.

- If your child is having difficulties learning to blow, have him blow bubbles in front of a mirror so your child can see what his mouth needs to do to create the bubbles.

Purpose

- **Visual skills:** Since this activity requires your child to keep his eyes on the bubbles, it works on smooth eye tracking and also quick eye movements for scanning (saccades), which helps develop the small muscles of the eyes.
- **Visual-perceptual input:** To scan the environment for the bubbles and then keep both eyes focused on the bubbles to track them, your child must differentiate the foreground information (bubbles) from the varying background information.
- **Eye-hand coordination:** Your child must visually track the bubble and then respond motorically by catching it with a wand, pinching it, or poking the bubble in midair.
- **Turn taking:** Use simple social language to work on pronouns: "my turn" and "your turn."
- **Body awareness:** You (the adult) call for popping the bubbles on the knee, nose, elbow, or head.
- **Language:** Work on descriptive concepts and quantity concepts, such as "big bubble" and "small bubbles."
- **Oral-motor control and breath support:** Maintaining an O shape with the lips while blowing requires the control of mouth muscles. Controlled, continuous blowing required to blow bubbles increases breath support, essential for voice projection.
- **Motor planning:** Chasing and popping the bubbles requires motor planning.
- **Social skills:** This game involves social reciprocity and shared enjoyment of "popping" the bubbles and taking turns.

GAME ⑥ Hidden Gems

Indoor/Outdoor

- Either

Equipment

- Sand in large plastic container or an outside sandbox (alternative: rice, beans, or small pastas in large plastic bins if doing the activity inside, or lots and lots of shaving cream in a baking pan)
- Items of high interest to your child, such as cars from the Lightning McQueen series, plastic figures, and so on (The key to this game is to use highly motivating items so your child will want to search for the items.)

How

- Hide the items in the sand, and go on a digging hunt for all the hidden "gems."
- Tell (show with your fingers if needed) how many gems are hidden in the sand. Then say, "There are five cars hidden in the

sand: Sally, Lightning, Doc, Mater, and Ramone. Can you find all five?"

- Encourage your child to bury his hands and arms into the sand to search for the objects, instead of moving the sand aside.
- Talk about each object your child finds.
- Have him place each object he finds into a container so he can "keep count."

Note: If you are inside and do not have time to create an indoor sandbox, hide small objects of high interest in shaving cream on a cookie sheet. If your child is resistant to touching the shaving cream, have him use a wooden craft stick to find the hidden gems. Another indoor option is to use a deep plastic container, fill it halfway with rice or beans, and hide the objects in it. If you have the room, you can get one big enough for your child to sit in while searching.

Purpose

- **Tactile registration:** Exposing your child to different media helps the child register tactile information, which is essential for discrimination.
- **Tactile discrimination:** By searching for the objects in the sand, which provides a lot of tactile input to the skin, he must use his discriminative tactile system to distinguish the sand from the objects he is searching for.
- **Tactile desensitization:** Searching for objects in tactilely rich materials helps desensitize the child who is touch sensitive, preparing the child for functional and academic activities such as buttoning and writing.
- **Preacademic skills:** This activity encourages your child to find a certain number of items that you can vary each time you play the game, thus encouraging numerical one-to-one correspondence.

This is a breakthrough activity; that is, you know that children are working past some of their sensory issues when they will put their hands and arms into the sand, rice, or shaving cream to get what they want. I have seen children go from literally gagging when they see any material that is tactilely stimulating to wanting to get their whole body in it. This is always a great sign that the touch system is moving past being in a constant defensive state and the discriminative system can begin doing its job.

> **WHY** Using highly motivating objects such as the characters of a favorite movie, show, or book, or little plastic animals that your child already identifies with is key to getting your child to play in tactile-rich media such as sand, shaving cream, or rice. Exposure to varying media increases tolerance of tactile input and leads to tactile registration as well as tactile desensitization, depending on the needs of your child's nervous system.

GAME ⑦ Swinging Eyes

Indoor/Outdoor

- Either

Equipment

- 4-inch by 6-inch white note cards
- A swing, if available

How (First Level)

- Draw different colored shapes on the cards. For instance, draw a red circle on one and a yellow triangle on another. Mix and match the color and shape combinations so there are no duplicates.
- If your child is at reading level, write large letters in different colors on the cards.
- Stand 10 feet away from your child, and have the child log-roll on the ground (arms to the side and body straight as the child rolls toward you). Make sure your child is on a comfortable surface so she will not get hurt.
- While the child rolls toward you, hold up different cards and encourage the child to call out the color and shape or the color and letter as she rolls.

Note: If your child won't log-roll, have the child spin around twice and then yell out what she sees on the card. Another approach is to stand behind your child and have her stand with legs apart and drop her head between her legs. Then in that position, the child calls out the colors, shapes, and letter combinations on the cards.

How (Second Level)

- Have the child swing back and forth on the swing. Hold up different cards the same way you did in the first level, and have your child again identify what is on each card.
- Now try another activity by having the child spin on the swing and call out the colors, shapes, and letter combinations on the cards.

Purpose

- **Visual-vestibular integration:** This is an active way to promote integration of your child's vestibular and visual systems. The two must work together to control the eyes so they can fixate on the card while the head is in motion.

■ **Occular-motor control:** This activity requires eye pursuits and smooth tracking movements to track a still object while the body is moving.

■ **Preacademic skills:** Color, shape, and letter recognition is reinforced.

■ **Sensory modulation:** The nervous system must register the powerful vestibular input and modulate reactions to it so the brain can attend to the recognized visual pattern and verbally respond to it.

WHY The vestibular system controls the small muscles of the eyes. Therefore, the vestibular and visual systems working together play a large role in ocular-motor control. It is important for children to engage in activities that require integration of both systems. This activity forces the eye to fixate while the head is moving. This is an essential skill when engaging in active sports, such as following the ball to kick it ahead in soccer, or even for something as basic to a child's survival as running across the play yard to Mom.

GAME (8) Crashing Towers

• •

Indoor/Outdoor

■ Outdoor

Equipment

- A sandbox or a large, shallow plastic container filled with sand
- Different sizes of plastic cups
- Duplicate pairs of your child's favorite characters in a small form (half the size of the child's hand) such as Lightning McQueen, SpongeBob, Thomas the Tank Engine, Dora, or others

How

- Fill the cups with sand. Then place one of each duplicate character pairs in a cup of sand. Pack the sand.
- Then both you and your child make sand towers in the box by turning over the cups of packed sand.
- The first few times, have the child watch you place one of the duplicate characters in the cup of sand so the child knows that the character is in a sand tower. Keep the second duplicate of each pair off to the side—these do not go in the sand.
- After the first few times, put the character in the cup while the child is building the other towers, so he does not see which sand tower the character is in, this will make it more challenging.
- Take the second duplicate of a pair, and tell your child, for example, that SpongeBob needs to find his match.
- Now comes the guessing part. Have the character sit on top of each tower, and ask, "Is his friend in here?"
- Then encourage the child to smash the sand tower to find out who is hiding in it.

Purpose

- **Tactile acclimation:** This game encourages immersion in a tactile activity that acclimates a child to "touch sensory information."
- **Upper-extremity strength:** Packing the towers requires upper-extremity shoulder, arm, and hand strength to pack the sand into the cups.

- **Visual memory:** Because your child has to try to remember which sand tower the character is hidden in, he has to use visual attention and memory.

> **WHY** As said previously, some children with neurological difficulties are tactilely defensive. Children who have tactile defensiveness have difficulty touching different textures and are resistant to activities that require touch. So using characters that a child likes to encourage sand play is a way to desensitize a child to touch, which will carry over to other touch activities.

GAME (9) Gak 'n' Cars

Indoor/Outdoor

- Either, close to a sink or hose

Equipment

- 1 cup glue
- 1 cup cornstarch
- Spoon with large handle
- Bowl used for mixing ingredients for a cake
- Food coloring (optional)
- Water
- Cookie sheet or a flat container
- Small cars about 2 inches long

How

- Place glue in the bowl, add cornstarch, and stir with the spoon until the mixture thickens to a sandlike consistency. Add food coloring if you like. Use the water to lessen thickness if necessary.
- Have your child use the spoon to scoop the mixture onto a cookie sheet, coating the bottom of the sheet. Smooth the mixture out, using the spoon.
- Have your child try to move the cars from one end of the cookie tray to the other.

Note: More than one child can participate in this activity, and the children can race the cars from end to end.

Purpose

- **Tactile input:** Gak is the most gooey tactile material I can think of. This is a fun way to have children get their hands in a wet, sandlike medium to provide tactile input.
- **Upper-extremity strength:** This is a sticky substance, so mixing it in a large bowl requires strength of the shoulder, arm, and wrist.
- **Bilateral coordination:** To mix these ingredients, your child must stabilize the mixing bowl with one hand while mixing with the other hand.

WHY This activity provides the ultimate in touch input for children with tactile sensitivities, but because they get to be part of the "making" phase, they are more likely to engage in the touch phase even if they are defensive. Also, since the car is a conduit to touching the gak, your child won't see the prospect of the touch input as threatening.

GAME ⑩ Sensory Box

....

Indoor/Outdoor

- Either

Equipment

- A cardboard box at least 24 inches by 18 inches by 24 inches (moving boxes)
- String, Ping-Pong balls, packing peanuts, torn paper, torn pieces of cloth, large pieces of pasta, popcorn
- Sponges

How

- Make sure the child is part of every process.
- Cut multiple pieces of string into lengths varying from 12 to 18 inches.
- Cut holes in the side of the box to allow for a person to crawl in, and punch holes in the top of the box.
- Attach the string inside the box with the balls, rags, torn pieces of paper, pasta, and popcorn hanging from them—but only a few at first.
- Place cut-up sponges of various sizes along with the packing peanuts on the floor of the box.
- Have the child crawl into the box through the hanging strings.
- Increase the number of hanging strings as the child becomes more accustomed to the sensation.

Purpose

- **Vestibular input:** This is a safe way to acclimate your child to entering into different spaces, since your child has the ability to control moving in and out of the space.

- **Tactile input:** Crawling through the strings with various textures attached will decrease sensitivity to tactile input.
- **Bilateral control:** Stringing the various textured items to the box requires bilateral control.
- **Activity control:** Since the child helps throughout the process of creating the sensory box, she will feel more in control of entering the space.

Note: I did this project with a group of three boys. One of the boys was very tactile defensive and at first refused to take part in stringing the different materials. Instead he watched the other two boys do it. One day, when we were putting everything in the box, he requested to "do his own string." He turned a corner that day, stringing old washrags and then holding the string up and showing all of us. I knew it was going to be hard for him to go in the box and have all that sensory input around him in a small space, but he did it. The other two boys even clapped when he went in.

WHY Many children with sensory processing difficulties are fearful of small spaces and new sensory environments, mainly due to vestibular processing deficits since they may not be able to register and "make sense" of the new spatial information quickly. Giving them control over the environment, even if it is a small one, will give them greater confidence in other situations. Also, by being part of the preparation of the different textures that will be included in the box, they will have already experienced the textures with their hands. So they will be more comfortable having those textures touch other parts of their bodies.

GAME ⑪ Magnifying Glass Search

Indoor/Outdoor

- Either, but preferably outdoor

Equipment

- Cardboard or poster board
- Scissors
- Plastic stretch wrap
- Glue

How

- Using cardboard or poster board, create a large magnifying glass by cutting a hole in the cardboard about 6 inches in diameter (note: you do not want your child's head to fit through it) and leaving a handle at one end.
- Place the plastic stretch wrap over the hole, securing it to the cardboard with the glue.
- Have the child stand in a fixed spot. You can use a hula hoop to indicate where to stand.
- Instruct the child to scan the area through the magnifying glass, looking for three objects that you decide upon, such as a rock, tree, flower, and so on.

Note: If you are indoors, place familiar objects around the room in unexpected places such as a fork on a shelf, Thomas the Train on a chair, or a cup on a television.

Purpose

- **Visual skills:** This activity encourages eye convergence because your child's eyes have to work together to scan across the room, as well as visual skills such as pursuits and saccades.
- **Visual processing:** This activity requires visual discrimination, especially discrimination of foreground versus background information.
- **Attention/observation skills:** This activity promotes attention skills since it enables your child to focus on the task at hand with a physical prompt that enhances visual focus by blocking some of the potential field of vision, leading to less distraction.

> **WHY** Visual skills allow a child to scan across a room, track a moving object, or keep both eyes together (visual convergences) so that they can smoothly move across the words on a page, as well as help us negotiate around moving objects or people. Visual skill deficits inhibit children in academic settings and lead to fear reactions in visually busy situations. This magnifying glass activity works on eye convergence because the field the children can look through has been limited, thus prompting the eyes to work together to scan across the room.

GAME ⑫ Lycra Swing

Indoor/Outdoor

- Indoor

Equipment

- A bolt of Lycra (buy at fabric store) approximately 3 feet wide and 3 yards long with the ends sewn together in the long direction to create a ring (Swimsuit Lycra works well. It is expensive but very sturdy.)

How

- For very young children, a single adult can create a swing by holding the Lycra in the longer direction to create a hammock effect.
- For slightly older children, two adults are needed. Grab the ends of the Lycra to create a hammock.
- Make sure the child is secure in the Lycra, and gently swing child back and forth. If your child appears to be enjoying the movement, you can add a rotary component and swing your child in a circular motion. (Don't do it more than a couple of times, because it may make you dizzy and thus less stable while swinging your child.)
- For a child who is afraid of swings, place the Lycra on the ground and have her sit on the Lycra. You and another adult gently lift the ends, raising the child slightly off the ground. I have seen so many children adjust to the movement and even enjoy it when it is introduced in conjunction with the proprioceptive input from the Lycra.

Purpose

- **Vestibular input:** Suspended equipment such as a swing provides the most powerful input to the vestibular system.
- **Proprioceptive input:** Lycra provides deep pressure to the body, which has a calming effect on the nervous system.
- **Calming effect:** The back-and-forth rhythmic movement of the swing has a calming effect on the nervous system and can be an

effective part of a daily routine for children who constantly feel overstimulated.

- **Alerting behavior:** Rotary movement—spinning the child or moving in a circle—has an alerting effect on the nervous system.

> **WHY** Vestibular input is the most powerful input to your child's sensory nervous system. It can also elicit fear reactions because it is such a dominant sense. Pairing proprioceptive input provided by the Lycra, which has a calming effect on the nervous system, with vestibular input allows your child to experience this type of movement with a greater feeling of safety.

GAME ⑬ Musical Pillows

Indoor/Outdoor

- Indoor

Equipment

- Large pillows or couch cushions
- Audio equipment with music

How

- The game is played much like musical chairs, except that the pillows do not get removed from the game. You can play this game with one child or a few.
- Place the large pillows or couch cushions in a circle, at least 2 feet apart.

- Start the music, and direct the children to march or dance around the pillows while the music is playing.
- Have each child fall on one empty pillow when the music stops, taking care not to fall on a pillow that someone else has fallen on. (Control when the music stops.)
- For older children, one of the participants can choose to control the music.

Note: I use this activity with small groups of children who typically don't have the skills to initiate play with each other. After a few times of stopping and starting the music, I can't help but get caught up in how much fun they are having with their own bodies and inadvertently with each other. The hard part of this activity is being able to stop it once you get the kids started!

Purpose

- **Motor response to auditory input:** Jumping on a pillow on cue requires motor reaction to auditory cues.
- **Proprioceptive input:** Falling on pillows provides a tremendous amount of deep pressure to the entire body. Children are able to grade the amount of pressure they seek in this activity by the amount of force they use to jump or lie on the pillow when the music stops.
- **Socialization:** It is easy to incorporate peers into this game (think play date) because it does not have strict rules or much reciprocal receptive language. Since your child is doing it with others, the child learns to be cognizant of others by not falling on the same pillow as the other participants. Also, the child benefits from being jointly engaged in an activity with the same objective as the other participants without the stress of competition.

WHY Linking music to movement helps increase engagement in a movement activity. It also allows children to predict upcoming movements and increases internal timing and rhythm, which are linked to vestibular-auditory integration.

GAME (14) Swinging Crane

Indoor/Outdoor

- Indoor

Equipment

- Barbeque tongs
- Swing that is set approximately 18 inches from the ground (The swing needs to be a platform big enough to allow the child to lie on her belly. Precaution: make sure there is a mat under the swing large enough to cover any area that a child might fall onto. Also be sure that your child has sufficient balance to stay on the swing.)
- Simple objects such as beanbags and favorite small toys

How

- Set up the objects on the mat in close proximity to the swing.
- Put the child on her belly with her arms off the swing, facing in the forward swinging direction.
- Slowly push the swing.
- Instruct her to pick up the objects using the tongs as she swings.

Note: Since most people do not have a therapy swing in their house, you can modify this activity by using a therapy ball (a large exercise ball). Your child lies on her belly on the ball; you hold the child's legs and slowly move them back and forth while the child tries to pick up the objects.

Purpose

- **Vestibular input:** Swinging provides one of the most powerful types of vestibular input.
- **Visual scanning:** The child must quickly scan the visual field to locate the objects to pick up during the activity.
- **Eye-hand coordination:** Picking up the items with the tongs requires the eye teaming with the hands, as well as timing.
- **Fine motor:** The child must grasp the small objects; the smaller the objects, the more refined the fine motor coordination needs to be.

Note: To add more of a visual-perceptual component to this activity, you can throw small stuffed animals in with the beanbags and ask the child to pick up only the stuffed animals or ask for the beanbags of a particular color. This increases the visual-perceptual demand of the activity, requiring increased figure-ground versus foreground processing.

WHY Vestibular processing is a challenge for many children, and suspended equipment such as a swing offers the most powerful vestibular input. This swinging activity offers a robust way to stimulate the vestibular system while at the same time challenging fine and gross motor coordination as well as visual skills and visual-motor integration.

GAME ⑮ Noise to My Ears

Indoor/Outdoor

- Indoor

Equipment

- Audio equipment for recording and playing back auditory material (e.g., a simple audiocassette player)
- Recordings of about fifteen sounds that are familiar to your child—some she enjoys and some she might be a little scared of
- Pictures of the things that make the fifteen sounds on the recordings

How

- Record everyday sounds, including some sounds that your child enjoys and some that cause her fear.
- Lay out the pictures on a table.
- Play the sound recordings. Be sure to have a 20-second delay between each sound.
- Have the child choose to the best of her ability which picture is associated with each sound as it is played.

Purpose

- **Auditory sensitivity:** This activity is designed to reduce sensitivity through repeated exposure to sound as well as the association of the original source of the sound.
- **Auditory discrimination:** This is a rudimentary way to have children discriminate different sounds and their sources.

WHY One of the behaviors most commonly reported by parents is adverse reactions to everyday sounds. Since part of the fear of the sound is the inability to locate where the sound is coming from and what is causing it, having the child associate the sound with its source during a fun game may help the child learn to generalize his or her understanding of the sound and decrease fear reactions in the natural environment.

GAME ⑯ Blowing Races

Indoor/Outdoor

- Indoor

Equipment

- Any table
- Cotton balls, Ping-Pong balls, or even grains of rice
- Straws of different lengths and widths

How

- Make your table into a racetrack.
- Line up cotton balls or other race materials, and show your child how to blow them across the table.
- Try blowing through straws of different lengths and widths.

Purpose

- **Ocular-motor control:** To know where the cotton ball is, your child will have to converge his eyes at a near distance.

- **Breath support:** This activity requires increased breath support to continue blowing the item across the table.
- **Oral-motor control:** Your child must purse her lips around the straw to blow through the straw.

> **WHY** Eye convergence is essential for reading, since it is a prerequisite for binocular vision and eye tracking. Children who struggle neurologically often struggle with ocular-motor control, so infusing activities that support controlled movement of the small muscles of the eyes sets your child up for effective reading.

GAME ⑰ Assembly Line

Indoor/Outdoor

- Either

Equipment

- Scooter board
- Containers (coffee-can size and various sizes)
- Small items your child can hold in his hand, such as plastic coins, poker chips, or even marbles

How

- Create a path on a flat floor surface, indoors or outdoors, by lining up containers of various sizes about 3 feet apart widthwise so that between the containers there is a visual path. The short buckets or coffee-can-sized containers should be placed about every 4 to 5 feet from each other going down the path. Tell your child that you are setting up an assembly line. He will be in charge of putting the small items into the containers, and each container needs only one item.

- Position the scooter board at the beginning of the path.
- Have your child lie on his belly on the scooter board with his shoulders just off the surface of the scooter board.
- Have your child hold several of the small items in each hand.
- Hold your child's feet and start to push him down the path from behind.
- He must keep his arms and hands up while being pushed and drop only one item into each bucket along the path.
- Go back and count how many buckets he successfully dropped one item inside.

Purpose

- **Gross motor coordination:** You child must maintain a grasp on the items while keeping the arms extended in front of the head, ready to put the items in the containers.
- **Visual-motor integration:** While moving, your child must coordinate his body into position to successfully drop the items into the containers.
- **Visual skills:** The eyes must take in information in the central and peripheral visual fields while moving.

WHY This type of multisensory activity prepares children for the visual and vestibular-integrative skills required for day-to-day activities (moving around through a mall) as well as classroom demands. It requires a wide range of eye movement as well as visual-motor coordination while moving in a different plane (horizontal) than is typical. Also, it requires that the child's eyes move between central vision and peripheral vision.

GAME ⑱ Scooter Board Crash

Indoor/Outdoor

- Indoor

Equipment

- Scooter board
- Large, soft pillows (couch-seat-cushion size)

How

- Have your child lie on her belly on the scooter board.
- Put the pillows against the wall and in a pile in front of the wall. Be sure to have sufficient padding; test it yourself by rolling into the pillows.
- Make sure the child keeps her arms off the ground. Cue the child verbally, saying something like, "Keep your arms up like Superman."
- Grab your child's feet (while they are on the scooter board), and push her toward the pillow pile.
- Let go of your child's feet just before getting to the pile, and let your child crash into the pillows.

Purpose

- **Proprioceptive input:** Crashing into the pillows will provide deep proprioception input, which helps increase body awareness.
- **Gross motor skills:** Keeping the head upright while on the scooter board promotes strengthening of the deep and superficial extensor muscles.
- **Vestibular input:** Moving the body and head in a different plane (horizontally) than is typical increases vestibular integration.

> **WHY** It is hard for children with vestibular processing difficulties to move out of the vertical plane. So to entice your child to move in the horizontal plane have the "reward" of crashing into big, soft pillows, some of the vestibular sensitivity can be modulated.

3

GROSS MOTOR SKILLS

WHEN WE THINK about gross motor skills, we usually think of walking, running, and jumping. What many people do not realize is that there is more to gross motor skills than the simple act of moving. Gross motor skills rely on effective sensory processing of a number of different skills and systems, especially the body senses: tactile, proprioceptive, and vestibular processing. They also require an understanding of the properties of our physical world. Coordinated gross motor actions also call for sufficient muscle tone, trunk control, and muscle strength. If all of this is present, then the key to "good" gross motor skills is effective motor planning.

Praxis (referred to as motor planning) is the bridge between brain processing and motor control—it's the process where the brain tells the body to do something, which results in the body actually doing it. There are three stages of praxis: ideation, motor planning, and execution. The communication between the brain and body allows us to accomplish new tasks as well as familiar tasks in new environments confidently. For example, the simple act of picking up a rattle is quite complicated. When you watch a baby learning to reach for an object, you are privy to a conversation between the brain and the body that goes something like this:

■ **Your infant's eyes:** "Hey, brain, you should see this new object (rattle). I haven't seen anything like this before."

■ **Brain:** "Let's check it out and get a little more information from the hands. You guys up for it?"

■ **Hands:** "Let's do it, but how?"

■ **The brain:** "You, me, and the eyes up there need to work together. Trunk muscles, wake up! We need you to help us stay upright."

■ **The eyes:** "Hey, brain, tell the hand to move forward."

The brain transfers information to the hand. The hand reaches and misses. The eyes tell the brain that the hand reached too far.

■ **The hand:** "Hey, bad coordination, you two."

■ **The brain:** "OK, arm, it's a little closer to us, so tighten your muscles and bend your elbow."

If there's a glitch in the wiring of the motor planning system, new skills do not easily move from conscious control to automatic control. The child whose brain and body do not plan and execute together, in essence struggling with praxis, must expend much cognitive energy trying to figure out how to physically interact in his or her environment. You will often hear therapists refer to a child's struggles with praxis as dyspraxia.

Furthermore, many children who have praxis difficulties do not readily generate ideas that would spur them to interact in their world. The motor planning system stores a library of basic skills that it can rely on as a foundation comprising the entire middle shelf of your child's Brain Library. This allows the body and brain to learn more complex skills without having to attend to the basic stored skills. For example, the child whose motor planning system shelves are well stacked with bilateral skill experiences will look through a play yard, see his friend at the top of the playscape, run full-steam ahead, wind around the girls playing jump rope, continue to run under the football being tossed between two older boys, slow down just enough to put his right foot on the first step of the playscape, and join his friend at the top with their secret handshake. The child with praxis difficulties may want to get to the top of the playscape but would not have any idea of how to plan to navigate around the obstacles on the play yard, people, or objects. When he makes the attempt, he may find himself running into things or people and requiring much more time to get to his goal. One of the sure signs that a child is struggling with praxis is when the child always moves to the back of the line as children are lining up for a physical activity. Another example is the child who obviously wants to play, but because of these difficulties, he will walk the perimeter of the playground because he does not know how to enter into a game.

Dyspraxia, or difficulties with motor planning, can be seen in difficulties with gross motor, fine motor, and speech skills since they all rely on intact sensory processing and motor control. Thus it is not uncommon for a child with motor-planning difficulties to struggle with gross and fine motor skills as well as the motor control required for smooth speech. Motor planning references the base sensory systems while pulling the cognitive and motor system together; it lays the foundation for higher-level academic skills. This is one reason engaging your child in activities geared to learning gross motor skills is a powerful starting point for the development of other skills.

GAME ⑲ Jumpin' Bears

Indoor/Outdoor

- Indoor, but can be outdoor

Equipment

- Mini-trampoline
- Container of small rubber, multicolored bears or a couple of small stuffed animals

How (First Level)

- Place a small number of same-colored bears on the trampoline.
- Be sure your child has her shoes on for this activity.
- Then hold your child's hands and say, "Show the bears how to jump." You may need to physically cue your child to jump.
- Once she is jumping, encourage her to keep jumping until all the bears have "jumped off."

How (Second Level)

- Put two different-colored bears on the trampoline, and have your child yell out the color of the bear that is jumping off, such as "Yellow bear!" or "Red bear!" Some children will simply jump up and down, watching the bears fly off the trampoline. After they hear you say, "Yellow bear is jumping off!" or "Red bear is jumping off!" over and over, they will start to identify the color of the bear jumping off the trampoline.

■ Most children will modify their jumping (jump slower, change placement of feet during landing, etc.) as they try to figure out how to make the remaining bears jump off the trampoline.

■ For added fun, sing the song, "Five Little Monkeys Jumping on the Bed," but substitute *bears* for *monkeys* in the song.

Note: For a younger child, start with one small stuffed bear on the trampoline while the child is jumping and say, "Bear is jumping off the trampoline." Once he understands the concept of the game, you can try the smaller rubber bears.

Purpose

■ **Motor planning:** Since the child has to think about *how* to jump to get the bears to bounce off, the activity requires increased motor planning.

■ **Visual tracking:** Watching the bears jump off requires following the bears' movements as they "jump off."

■ **Proprioception:** Jumping on a trampoline increases deep-pressure input to the body, which has an integrating, calming impact on the nervous system.

■ **Vestibular-visual integration:** The child uses his eyes to scan while his feet are off the ground.

■ **Preacademic skills:** This activity fosters color recognition and identification.

■ **Language:** This activity builds concepts such as "off" and "jumping."

Note: Although this activity provides much sensory-type input, I first thought of it many years ago when a speech therapist asked me to cotreat a four-year-old boy with her. She had been working with him for several months, and he was not gaining new words. She was looking for different ways to get him to talk. I did this activity with him and really overemphasized the "language" component of it. After a few sessions, the speech therapist and I couldn't believe the verbal leaps he was making while bouncing on the trampoline.

> **WHY** Simply jumping on a trampoline allows a child to bounce, providing proprioceptive stimulation. However, requiring the child to bounce the bears off the trampoline means the child must change his or her motor movement and plan how to jump in more strategic ways to meet the objective of the game.

GAME ⑳ Floating Balloon

Indoor/Outdoor

- Either

Equipment

- Large balloons

How (First Level)

- Bat a balloon back and forth a few times at first until your child gets the concept of the game.

- Then integrate peers. Have all participants hit the balloon to keep it afloat as long as possible.
- For added challenge, the adult calls out which hand the children should use to hit the balloon.
- Another possible challenge is to add a second colored balloon. The adult calls out which colored balloon should be hit.

How (Second Level)

- Have the children play balloon soccer, where they use their knees and their head to keep the balloon afloat. This is geared toward older children because it requires more motor coordination and is more physically taxing as well.
- The advanced activity requires and stimulates core strength and is much more motivating than sit-ups.

Purpose

- **Trunk rotation:** This activity requires trunk rotation to turn and hit the balloon.
- **Readying response:** A key to gross motor coordination is readying the body to respond to things or people moving around it.
- **Visual tracking:** This activity requires the eyes to track a moving object.
- **Eye-hand coordination:** This activity promotes basic motor response to incoming visual information.
- **Bilateral control:** This activity requires the child to use both sides of the body to hit the balloon.
- **Physical endurance:** Keeping the shoulders and arms elevated for extended periods of time helps promote physical endurance.
- **Trunk stability:** Keeping the arms in an extended position, as well as being fluid in responding and batting the balloon, requires and promotes trunk stability.
- **Socialization:** This is another game that promotes interaction without requiring the child to follow specific rules. It also allows

children who struggle with language skills to participate in an interactive game with a peer.

- **Auditory integration:** The child must integrate the auditory information and translate it into motor action.

> **WHY** Many children in this population exhibit low muscle tone, which impacts their endurance as well as motor coordination during everyday activities. This activity offers a fun way to strengthen the deep muscles of the core and promotes shoulder stability. Both are essential for sitting in the classroom and writing.

How (Third Level)

- Child keeps a balloon afloat while bouncing on the trampoline.

Purpose

- **Vestibular input:** Bouncing on the trampoline challenges the vestibular system.
- **Proprioception:** Bouncing provides cyclic deep input, which gives the body increased input to the joints about where your body is in relation to itself.

> **WHY** The trampoline is a medium to heighten the sensory input to the body through the vestibular and proprioceptive systems. The processing of these two systems lays a basis for more effective motor planning. Although the game is harder relative to when your child is standing on the ground, it is possible to carry out this activity because the bouncing has put the vestibular and proprioceptive systems on high alert.

GAME ㉑ Lycra Ring

....

Indoor/Outdoor

- Either

Equipment

- A bolt of Lycra (buy at fabric store) approximately 3 feet wide and 9 feet long, with ends sewn together creating a ring (Swimsuit Lycra works well. It is expensive but very sturdy.)
- Beach ball

How

- Spread the Lycra out into a ring so you and your child can get in the Lycra circle with the beach ball close at hand.
- Have your child step in first. Pull the Lycra up so that it is wrapped around your child's shoulders and back. Then get into the Lycra circle as well.
- You and your child should back away from each other until the Lycra is pushing against each of your bodies. The idea is to keep pressure against the Lycra.
- Encourage your child to gently kick the ball to you while still pressing back against the Lycra.

Note: This game can include a few children. For younger children who do not have kicking skills yet, have one child sit at one end of the Lycra circle and the other child at the other end so the Lycra is stretched tight around their shoulders and backs. They will need to sit with their legs in an open V. Then have them push a ball back and forth to each other. This is a less scary way of playing ball activities, the ball is in the same plane as the child's eyes.

Purpose

■ **Spatial awareness:** The Lycra ring acts a physical boundary, decreasing the space in which your child can operate his body.

■ **Proprioceptive/touch input:** The entire time the child is engaged in the activity, he is giving himself physical input and helping draw his attention inward. The Lycra acts as a nonthreatening boundary. It is akin to touching a child on the shoulder to let him know that the ball is heading his way.

■ **Bilateral control:** By requiring your child to stabilize and balance on one foot while kicking the ball with the other, this activity requires bilateral coordination of the lower extremities.

■ **Visual scanning:** Your child must visually track the ball as it rolls across the floor.

■ **Visual-motor skills:** Your child must coordinate his body's timing and response to make successful contact and kick the ball.

WHY Due to their multisensory nature, ball activities are something that many children with autism, Asperger's, or sensory processing disorder find too difficult to do. This is because such games require visual tracking, a motor response, and attention. Using the Lycra ring as a stabilizer and boundary helps provide support to the trunk and the pelvic girdle while the child is standing and to the entire trunk area while the child is sitting because many children with neurological difficulties have low muscle tone. Low muscle tone refers to lack of tension in the muscles, which is linked to low muscle strength.

GAME ㉒ Scooter Safari

■■■

Indoor/Outdoor

- Indoor

Equipment

- Square scooter board
- Small toy jungle animals (or laminated pictures or picture cards of animals)
- Cardboard box (The size of the box can vary depending on what you have available; however, you want to make sure it is big enough to accommodate all the animals coming to the zoo.)

How (First Level)

- Place the small toy animals (or laminated pictures or picture cards) around the room. Place the animals under, on, in, in front of, or behind objects in the room.
- You and your child should set up the cardboard box together and talk about how all the animals are going to come live in the zoo.
- Tell your child that she has to find all the animals and bring them to their new home.
- Have your child lie on the scooter board with her upper body extended off the scooter board. The edge of the scooter board should be just below the armpits, allowing the arms the freedom to move.
- Show your child how to propel herself on the board by physically by moving her arms in an alternating motion and thus pulling herself along on the scooter board. By using physical assistance to teach her how to move her arms, you are helping her motor plan her body. This will help increase the speed at which she is able to learn this new motor skill.

- As soon as the child reaches an animal, prompt the child to announce the animal, such as saying, "Tiger," or you can announce, "Tiger, you found the Tiger." Then, depending upon the child's level of language, prompt your child by saying, "Where was the tiger?" or say two to three times, "The tiger was under the table."
- Upon retrieving the animal, have your child bring it to the cardboard box (zoo) where the animals can live. She can walk back to the zoo and then go back to the scooter board.
- Then have your child get back on her scooter board to retrieve the next animal and bring it to its new home.

How (Second Level)

- Infuse language into the game by having your child identify the animal and make the animal sound. You may have to demonstrate the animal-and-sound combination a few times.

Purpose

- **Motor planning:** Encourage a child to decide how to move her arms so that she can navigate the room to get to the next object. This develops the child's thought process.
- **Strengthening:** This activity builds upper-extremity strength, specifically shoulder and arm strengthening.
- **Bilateral coordination:** Moving both hands together to propel the scooter board promotes bilateral coordination.
- **Vestibular input:** Changing the plane of the child's head in space from vertical to horizontal excites the vestibular system.
- **Direction following:** This activity is helpful for gaining command of multistep directions.
- **Proprioception:** This activity provides increased deep-pressure input to the upper extremities.

- **Visual-motor skills:** Visual skills (visual-perceptual and ocular-motor) are used to scan the environment room, perceive the animal of interest, and then fix on the animal as the child moves toward it.
- **Language:** This activity introduces the concepts of *on, under, behind, in front of,* and *in.* These concepts help increase the child's understanding when following directions and expand the child's vocabulary (animal names).

> **WHY** One of the significant benefits of crawling is the deep pressure provided to the palmar surface of the hands, which facilitates the arch formation of the hand. This is key to fine motor skills. However, many children with developmental delays do not spend enough time crawling, thus missing this intense input to the palmar surface of the hands and upper extremities. This activity mimics the benefits gained from crawling, including shoulder strength and stability.

GAME (23) "Biking" Through the Maze

Indoor/Outdoor

- Outdoor

Equipment

- Chalk
- Tricycle

How

- Using chalk, draw a zigzag path on the ground.
- Have your child navigate the path on the tricycle.
- Increase the difficulty over time by drawing paths with ever more turns and sharper turns.
- Increase the difficulty even more by drawing arrows instead of drawing a full path.

Purpose

- **Motor planning (praxis):** First your child must learn to pedal the tricycle. Once the skill for pedaling the tricycle becomes automatic, introduce the path. This will further challenge his body and brain because he will have to think about when and how to steer the tricycle in order to keep it on the path.
- **Strengthening:** This is an excellent activity for strengthening the pelvic region and legs.
- **Visual attention:** You are requiring the child to focus the eyes forward to follow the chalk path.
- **Vestibular input:** This activity is alerting to the vestibular system, since the child's feet are away from the ground while they are in motion.
- **Vestibular-visual integration:** By requiring the child to visually focus on the line while moving, the activity promotes the integration of the vestibular-visual systems.

> **WHY** Pulling a child's visual focus forward while moving is imperative for safety. When the child is moving, be it on a tricycle or simply walking, it is important that he attends visually to information in front of him so he can navigate around people and objects in the environment.

GAME (24) Beanbag Toss

....

Indoor/Outdoor

- Either

Equipment

- Six beanbags
- Bucket
- Any household chair

How (First Level)

- Place the bucket about 5 feet away from the front of the chair. Have the child walk around a chair. When the child gets to the front of the chair, have the child toss the beanbags into the bucket. Progressively get farther away with successful tosses into the bucket.

How (Second Level)

- Have the child walk in a straight line or figure eight about 10 feet from the bucket and attempt to toss the beanbags into the bucket, which remains in a fixed position.

How (Third Level)

- The child remains in a fixed place, and someone moves the bucket around in a pattern (either straight line or figure eight). Again, toss the beanbags into the moving bucket.

How (Fourth Level)

- Standing about 10 feet from the bucket, the child begins to move along a line, and you move the bucket along a parallel line.

Purpose

- **Motor planning:** This activity works on the execution phase of the praxis (last phase of motor planning). This is a more advanced motor activity that requires being able to throw a beanbag with graded force as well as appropriate directionality.
- **Visual-motor skills:** The activity requires tossing the beanbag based on changing visual information (length and direction).
- **Visual tracking:** This activity requires that the eyes track a moving object when the child is in a fixed position, as well as concentrate on the immobile object while the child is moving. Then it requires tracking an object while both the child and object are moving.
- **Visual fixation:** The child must focus on the bucket long enough to comprehend where the target is.

> **WHY** As previously mentioned, children with a neurological diagnosis often have difficulty with praxis and visual skills. This activity requires some basic skills such as throwing with a sense of direction. There are varying stages of difficulty, from simple through advanced, with each step offering greater challenges for motor planning and visual skills development.

GAME (25) Beanbag and Pillow Balance

Indoor/Outdoor

- Either

Equipment

- Beanbag
- Small couch pillow
- Nonbreakable item (book, folder, towel)

How (First Level)

- Have the child keep the beanbag balanced on his or her head while walking in a straight line.

How (Second Level)

- Increase the difficulty by having the child keep the pillow balanced on his or her head while walking in a straight line.

How (Third Level)

- Have the child walk heel to toe while balancing the pillow on his or her head while walking in a straight line.

How (Fourth Level)

- Have the child carry a nonbreakable item while balancing the pillow on his or her head while walking in a straight line.

Purpose

- **Motor planning:** Keeping the beanbag or pillow balanced on his head requires the child to coordinate his body while making postural adjustments to keep the pillow or beanbag in place.
- **Dynamic postural control:** This activity requires body control around the midline, which demands that the musculoskelatal system respond to the changes in the child's movement to keep him or her balanced. Midline is the invisible plane that separates a

person's right from left and is roughly located about where the nose is.

- **Vestibular input:** By adding a proprioceptive input to the head (via the beanbag/pillow), the vestibular-proprioceptive-visual systems must integrate to maintain balance.

> **WHY** Sometimes children move through their environment without thinking about their body. This activity increases sensory stimuli to the head and neck area, which elicits cognitive focus to maintain upright posture and steady movement.

GAME ㉖ Bucket Catcher

Indoor/Outdoor

- Either

Equipment

- Beanbags
- Bucket

How (First Level)

- This activity uses the same equipment as for the beanbag toss but has the opposite objective.
- Someone (an adult or peer) tosses the beanbag in the child's direction.
- The child uses the bucket to catch the beanbags in it.
- To make the game more challenging, increase the distance between the person tossing and the child catching.

Purpose

- **Visual-motor skills:** For the child to catch a beanbag with a bucket, the child's visual-motor system has to work properly. As the distance increases between the thrower and the child with the bucket, the game becomes harder because he must track the beanbag from even farther distances.
- **Motor planning:** The child must coordinate and position his body to capture the beanbag as it flies through the air. As the distance increases between the thrower and the child with the bucket, the game becomes harder because the beanbag travels faster.
- **Proprioception:** This activity requires muscle grading for the child to ready the body to position the bucket, as well as to respond to the force of the beanbag hitting the bucket.

> **WHY** For many children with processing deficits, moving objects coming toward them will often elicit a fear reaction, because they cannot judge the speed of the object or its distance from them. Thus it is impossible for them to catch the object and protect themselves from being hit. By giving them a bucket and tossing a familiar object such as a beanbag from a short distance, you create a situation that the child may perceive as being safer, since the object will not be traveling fast and the child knows the beanbag will not hurt even if it hits him.

GAME (27) Catching on the Eight

Indoor/Outdoor

- Either, but preferably outdoor

Equipment

- Chalk for outside, colored tape for inside
- Beanbags or textured balls
- Large bucket

How (First Level)

- If outside, use colored chalk to draw a figure eight about 10 feet long on the sidewalk or driveway.
- If inside, use colored tape to create a figure eight about 10 feet long.
- First have your child walk on the figure eight, making sure the child can actually walk the figure eight pattern (meaning walk through the middle and around)
- Once the child can walk the figure eight pattern, you can tell the child to keep her eyes on you while she walks the figure eight carrying the bucket. Toss the beanbags to the child and have her catch them in the bucket.

How (Second Level)

- Once the child understands the game, you can toss the bean-bags faster and even two at a time to really challenge the child. You can also add a bucket at one end of the figure eight that your child can toss the beanbags into while walking.
- You can make this game more complicated by drawing or tap-ing a large X in a different color at one point on the figure eight, noting the place from where the child has to throw the beanbag back to you. Increase the difficulty even more by having your child march or cross-crawl march (i.e., while walking, alternate touching each leg with the hand from the opposite side of the body) the figure eight.
- Peers can easily be integrated into this game.

- For an increased level of difficulty, have music playing and instruct the child to stop walking when the music stops.
- An alternative would be to have the child call out the color of the beanbag as it flies through the air.

Note: Last year a mom told me her son who had been coming to occupational therapy talked about this activity a lot. He became very motivated to get better at controlling his eyes while he moved. He did, and his teacher reported that he was better able to copy from a board, and his mother reported that he had gone from being the kid who could not hit the baseball to the kid who hit a few. But more important, he enjoyed the game because he was no longer afraid of the ball when it came toward him.

Purpose

- **Vestibular-visual integration:** Walking on the figure eight while visually tracking the tossed beanbags requires the child to simultaneously process and integrate visual and vestibular input.
- **Motor coordination:** Catching the beanbag requires motor coordination in addition to the vestibular-visual integration.
- **Auditory input and integration:** If you have the music playing, integrating auditory information in addition to the vestibular and visual information will challenge the nervous system further.

> **WHY** Children with neurological difficulties often find integrating two or three systems simultaneously to be challenging. Accomplishing this activity will require the integration of several sensory systems at once.

GAME (28) Action Fishing

Indoor/Outdoor

- Either

Equipment

- Cardboard fish about 3 inches in length (you can make these)
- Paper clips (any size)
- Computer with Internet connection and printer
- Small, flat magnets
- Fishing pole: cardboard tube from a paper towel roll, colored construction paper, a string about 36 inches in length

How

- Download from the Internet cartoonlike pictures and add corresponding words underneath (as many as possible); use pictures of animals: crab walks, bear crawls, bunny hop on one foot; use pictures of people: throw ball, jump, run, do push-ups, head, shoulders, knees, toes. Print the pictures.
- Tape or glue each picture to a cardboard fish. Attach a paper clip to each picture.
- To make the fishing pole, wrap construction paper around the cardboard tube. Tie the string to one end of the tube; the hanging end should be about 24 to 30 inches long. Tie a magnet to the end of the string.
- Place the pictures facedown on the floor.
- Have the child fish by getting the magnet at the end of the fishing pole to pick up the various pictured items; then have the child roll the fishing rod to reel in the fish.
- Have the child act out the picture he or she pulls.

Purpose

■ **Eye-hand coordination:** Locating and picking up the fish promotes eye-hand coordination.

■ **Wrist rotation:** Reeling in the fish using the cardboard tube requires wrist rotation.

■ **In-hand manipulation:** Moving the fishing rod around requires in-hand manipulation.

■ **Bilateral coordination:** Taking the fish off the rod with one hand while holding the rod with the other promotes the use of left and right sides simultaneously.

■ **Gross motor skills:** Acting out the pictures requires gross motor involvement.

> **WHY** Many children steer away from gross motor activities that they find too challenging. This fun activity encourages participation in varying activities, both ones they find easy and some they find more difficult.

GAME (29) Zoom Ball

Indoor/Outdoor

■ Outdoor

Equipment

■ Zoom Ball game (Pressman)
■ Therapy balls

How

- Each participant grips the handles, one in each hand so that the knuckles touch.
- Have the Zoom Ball rest against one participant's handles.
- Sit on therapy balls far enough apart so that the cord is taut (about 18 feet apart). This can also be done on the knees.
- The participant closest to the Zoom Ball starts by pulling his hands and arms apart, sending the ball zooming toward the other participant.
- The other participant does the same, sending the ball back.

Purpose

- **Gross motor skills:** The participants must move the upper extremities to get the Zoom Ball moving back and forth.
- **Visual-vestibular integration:** The vestibular system working in conjunction with the visual system tells your child how quickly the ball is coming toward him.
- **Visual-motor:** Responding to the moving ball requires visual motor timing.
- **Visual convergence:** As the ball moves toward your child, his eyes need to converge to maintain focus on the ball.

> **WHY** Ball activities are a great way to work on visual-vestibular integration along with motor planning. However, a lot of children with neurological difficulties struggle with ball activities and can become very frustrated by them. Nonetheless, because the Zoom Ball is on a string, it ensures that the child on the other end *will* receive the ball, thus increasing participation in a ball activity. Altering the the children's positions increases the motor planning challenge, while "working out" the core muscles.

Indoor/Outdoor

■ Outdoor if possible

Equipment

■ Five hand-sized beanbags of different colors with different letters on each (available at most educational supply stores, or use a marker to write on beanbags you already have)

■ Five circles (12-inch diameter) made from poster board of different colors, with letters on one side of the circles and different numbers on the other side (**Note:** when writing the letters on the circles, take care not to exactly duplicate the letter-color scheme of the beanbags.)

How (First Level)

This game has graduated levels of difficulty. You can increase the difficulty of this game by having ten numbered circles with letters on the opposite side (*A* through *J*).

■ Place the circles on the floor, and have all participants stand about 5 feet away from the circles.

■ Each participant throws a beanbag onto the circle that matches the color of the beanbag.

How (Second Level)

■ Each participant throws a beanbag onto the circle with the letter that corresponds to the letter on the beanbag.

How (Third Level)

- Flip the circles over to the side with the numbers.
- Each participant throws a beanbag from beanbag letter *A* to circle 1, from *B* to 2, and so on.

Purpose

- **Eye-hand coordination:** This activity has the child coordinate the appropriate grade of force and directionality to toss the beanbag to the correct spot based on the target.
- **Letter recognition:** This activity requires letter recognition for the child to throw the beanbag to the target.
- **Praxis on verbal command:** The directions are auditory and need to be integrated with the motor output.

> **WHY** Since processing difficulties are well documented in these children, it is hoped that involving them in an activity that incrementally requires more mental agility will allow them to maintain focus throughout the activity. This type of activity challenges children's attention, working memory, and visual processing.

GAME (31) Turtle Shell

Indoor/Outdoor

- Indoor

Equipment

- Pillowcase
- Beanbags (Start with six and add more based on child's strength.)

- Obstacle course items: household items, chairs, pillows, sofa
- Different colors of tape

How (First Level)

- Put the beanbags into the pillowcase and sew the pillowcase closed to create the "turtle shell."
- Have child get on all fours, and place the pillowcase on his back.
- Make an obstacle course using household items. Then have the child crawl through the course without dropping the "turtle shell."

How (Second Level)

- Using different colors of tape, create paths that cross over each other throughout the room.
- Let the child choose a tape color.
- Follow the preceding directions with the additional challenge of staying on the path of the chosen color (put a dot on the child's hand for his color if necessary).

Purpose

- **Motor planning:** This activity uses visual and proprioceptive clues to aid with motor planning.
- **Upper-extremity strength:** Crawling with the additional weight on the back helps increase shoulder girdle strength and stability.
- **Visual-motor coordination:** Navigating through the path requires visual-motor coordination.
- **Hand muscle development:** The deep pressure from crawling helps develop the arches of the hand.
- **Body awareness:** Crawling provides proprioceptive input, which increases body awareness; the "turtle shell" increases the proprioceptive input.

WHY Intense proprioceptive input to the body increases body awareness, which is a prerequisite for motor planning, especially in the ideation phase of motor planning. Proprioceptive input in the form of deep pressure helps increase body awareness, which is essential for the early stages of praxis (motor planning). It is important for children to have internal references of how their bodies move so they can learn how to move in different ways.

4

FINE MOTOR SKILLS

IT PROBABLY MAKES sense to most of us that fine motor skills are
crucial for many academic skills, such as writing and cutting on
a curved line, as well as a broad array of everyday activities such as
using both hands together to button and unbutton, manipulating
scissors while adjusting the paper to cut on a line, positioning your
hands and fingers for typing, holding a pen properly to write your
name, and moving a quarter in your hand to the tips of your fingers and putting it into the slot of a soda machine. Well-developed
fine motor skills rely on intact sensory systems, postural stability
and mobility, and good muscle tone.

Fine motor skills are fairly complicated if you think about what
is required to button a shirt. First we must have stability in our
trunk and shoulders. Assuming we have sufficient stability, our
arms are free to move away from our body. Our arms gain stability from the shoulder, and the hands gain stability from the arms.
Once the arms are stable, our wrists will adjust to put the hands
and fingers in a good position to manipulate a button. Both hands

must work together to pull the buttonhole open, while the other hand pushes the button through the hole. The hands and fingers are able to concentrate on manipulation because there is an inherent stabilization and mobility in the trunk and shoulders. Early gross motor activities such as crawling help develop the muscles of the upper extremities, shoulders, arms, and even the small muscles of the hands, which later allow us to handle this button.

A sequential order that begins with the development of the gross motor skills allows for the intricate fine motor skills. First come shoulder and wrist stabilization, then strong thumb development. (This allows a person to pinch two fingers together while displaying good arch formation in the hands and good strength of the hands and fingers and, most important, requiring intact tactile and proprioceptive processing.) As the child gains strength through the trunk and shoulder girdle, he or she starts to use the hands and fingers to perform manipulative activities. These manipulative activities increase finger dexterity and refine in-hand manipulation and coordination of the hands and fingers. As a child's manipulation skills continue to develop, the child increases his or her sensory development because the nervous system takes in more detailed information about the properties of the people and objects in the surrounding environment. It is essential that children with neurological difficulties who may avoid fine motor activities be encouraged to develop these skills in fun ways with various materials. Promoting your child's development of fine motor skills will lead to increased independence in everyday activities, making your morning routine easier.

GAME 32 Coins in the Piggy Bank

Indoor/Outdoor

- Indoor

Equipment

- Various denominations of coins
- Plastic storage container (soup-bowl sized or smaller) with a slit cut in the lid and the slit edges covered with a few layers of heavy tape or Velcro to smooth out the sharp edges (Velcro is better. Keep the rough side up.)

How

- Have your child pick up coins using the pincer grasp (thumb and index finger).
- Child places the coins in the plastic "piggy bank."
- Next put a coin in the palmar surface of the child's hand, and instruct your child to move the coin to the tips of the fingers without using the other hand, which must stay on the table.

Note: If your child continues to rake the coin using the whole hand instead of just the fingers, tell your child that the pinky and ring finger are going to sleep and the only three workers are the index finger, middle finger, and the thumb. Isolate the two other fingers by wrapping them in gauze or plastic adhesive bandages.

Purpose

- **Developing pincer grasp:** Picking up coins with the thumb and index finger promotes the pincer grasp.

- **In-hand manipulation:** The child must use the arches of the hand to control the coin without the assistance of the other hand.
- **Gross motor skills:** The shoulders must be stable so the arms can move away from the body in a controlled manner to allow for precise movement of the hands and fingers.

> **WHY** Many children with fine motor difficulties will resort to using an awkward whole-hand grasp because of lack of strength and coordination. Using a whole-hand grasp interferes with the development of more intricate fine motor skills. This activity forces the muscles of the hand to work in a coordinated way to move the coins.

GAME (33) Smashing Tees

Indoor/Outdoor
- Either

Equipment
- Golf tees
- Block of Styrofoam
- Plastic hammer
- Colored sticker dots

How (First Level)
- Lay the tees out on a table.

- Have your child pick up the tees using only one hand—the nondominant hand—and insert each tee into the Styrofoam.
- Instruct the child to use the plastic hammer to bang the tee all the way in with his dominant hand. Demonstrate how to do it if necessary.
- To increase the level of difficulty, have the child insert more than one tee at a time into the Styrofoam to be banged in.

Note: If your child is having difficulty pushing the tee into the Styrofoam due to lack of strength, you can do it for him until he can.

How (Second Level)

- Put sticker dots on the Styrofoam, and instruct your child to put the tees through the dots.
- You can also use different colored tees, and have your child match the color of the tees to the dots.

Purpose

- **Motor control:** Since the activity requires that your child control the hammer to swing it with sufficient speed and accuracy, banging the tees into the Styrofoam requires motor control of the hand.
- **Wrist strengthening:** Wrist strength is promoted by the action of hammering and pushing the tee into the Styrofoam.
- **Eye-hand coordination:** Hitting the top of the tee accurately with the hammer requires visual-motor integration.
- **Upper-extremity stabilization:** To move the hands away from the trunk, the child's shoulder girdle must be able to stabilize so the arm can extend out, allowing for distal control of the hands and wrists.

GAME (34) River Town

Indoor/Outdoor

■ Outdoor

Equipment

■ Box of sand, at least 2 feet square
■ Pitcher of water

How

■ Instruct the child to carve out a "riverbed" in the sandbox using her hand. (The child cannot use a shovel.) Provide a demonstration for the child who needs it. Tell the child that a favorite boat needs a river.
■ Have the child pour water into the channel and watch the water run through it.
■ Expand the game to build towns on either side of the riverbanks to elicit pretend play.

Purpose

■ **Arch formation:** Using the hand as a shovel promotes arch formation in the hand.

- **Tactile input:** The act of creating the riverbed will provide much tactile input via the sand. Then once the water is added, the tactile input will change because there will be sand, water, and mud.
- **Upper-extremity strengthening:** Pulling the hand through sand requires upper-extremity strength.
- **Wrist strengthening:** Pouring the pitcher of water promotes increased wrist strength.

> **WHY** By using a sensory activity in a very purposeful manner and adding the component of pretend play, you are still working on strength and fine motor coordination, but you are doing it in the context of play for typically developing children.

GAME ㉟ Dot Coloring

Indoor/Outdoor

- Indoor

Equipment

- Wikki Stix (sticky waxy strings that come in various colors)
- Do-A-Dot markers
- Poster board
- Easel

How

- Use the Wikki Stix to create simple shapes, such as a circle, on a piece of white paper.
- Choose a color for each shape (e.g., red for circle, blue for square); place at colored dot inside each shape.

- Have your child color each shape the same color as its dot; the idea is that all the color is inside the Wikki Stix shape.
- Then have your child remove the Wikki Stix, and show the child the remaining circle that she made.
- The next step is to make several different shapes on white poster board; then tape it on a wall or clip it to an easel, and color on the vertical surface.

Purpose

- **Visual-perceptual and visual-motor skills:** The purpose of this activity is to encourage visual-perceptual understanding of borders, and then to work on motor control by coloring in the borders.
- **Kinesthetic input:** Using Wikki Stix rather than simply an outline of a shape provides kinesthetic input of the shape boundaries, thus increasing your child's understanding of the borders as well as the likelihood that she will stay in the lines.
- **Motor control:** This activity teaches motor control of a writing instrument, using a bigger instrument.
- **Wrist position:** By writing on a vertical surface, the child's hand is in a natural writing position.

WHY It is difficult to color inside the lines when there are many other distracting black lines and there is no input, other than visual, to not go over the line. The use of the Wikki Stix solves this problem. Also, many children have difficulty learning and maintaining proper wrist-and-hand position while writing. Activities that mandate the wrist to be in a proper writing position (e.g., when on a vertical surface) will enable the learning of proper letter formation and will decrease the likelihood of fatigue by teaching correct writing position of hand and wrist.

GAME ㊱ Pickup Speed

Indoor/Outdoor

- Either

Equipment

- Tweezers and small tongs
- One or more of the following materials: raw rice, beans, beads, small strips of paper, small pieces of cloth, cotton balls
- Small toy dump truck
- A piece of dark-colored construction paper

Note: If there is any concern that your child will try to put the items in his mouth; use cereal as a substitute.

How

- Have the child pick up the small items by using the tongs or tweezers. (Show your child how to use the tongs or the tweezers; it is important that the child learns to use the thumb and first finger, especially when controlling the tweezers.)
- Have your child put the items in the toy dump truck.
- Have your child transport the items in the truck to the piece of construction paper and dump them out.
- Your child is done when the construction paper is covered (or almost covered).
- Keep in mind that the item's size will determine whether your child will use tongs or tweezers. Once your child understands the game and is able to use the tongs and tweezers, you can add a timed element. This game can be done while sitting at the kitchen table, or you can do it with your child and add a race component to it.

Purpose

- **Hand strength:** This activity helps develop grip strength, which is essential for handwriting and other fine motor tasks.
- **Thumb opposition:** This activity develops good thumb opposition to first finger (prerequisite for handwriting). Many of the activities shown in this book work on thumb-to-finger opposition; this activity specifically supports and encourages thumb opposition.
- **Attention:** This game requires that a child attend to the task and concentrate to complete it.
- **Sequencing:** The child must follow a three-step process throughout the game.

> **WHY** The muscles responsible for developing thumb-to-finger opposition are key to self-help skills. Children who have poor hand-to-thumb opposition have difficulties with handwriting, cutting, dressing, as well as other everyday tasks. Providing opportunities for your child to develop the muscles of the hand, specifically the three major muscles of the thenar eminence stabilizes the thumb which is crucial for developing other more refined skills.

GAME 37 Let It Rain

Indoor/Outdoor

- Indoor

Equipment

- Colored construction paper, large sheet of white paper
- Scissors
- Glue
- Easel, if available
- Plastic to put on the ground below the easel
- Glass jar (size of peanut butter jar)
- Blue food coloring
- Eyedropper

How

- Have the child cut out a simple shape, such as an umbrella, grass, or a tree, from the construction paper. (Keep it simple.) Alternatively: Cut out a car, and make this a car wash.
- Glue the shape to the white paper.
- Clip the shape onto an easel or tape it to a wall, but make sure to have a container and plastic below the paper.
- Mix water and a couple drops of blue food coloring in the jar.
- Pinch the eyedropper, and squeeze the blue water into the eyedropper.
- Show your child how to create rain on the umbrella, grass, flowers, and so on by squeezing the eyedropper to create the rain.
- Alternative: Using the eyedropper, your child can transfer colored water from a solid cup to clear cups where the child can see the different colored water; the key is to have the child transfer the water only with the eyedropper.

Purpose

- **Pincer grasp:** Pinching and releasing the eyedropper helps develop a pincer grasp. Your child may use his first and second fingers along with the thumb when learning to manipulate the eyedropper. However, as his strength increases, encourage him to use only the thumb and pointer.

- **Bilateral coordination:** Cutting out the umbrella or other shapes requires bilateral coordination, because your child has to stabilize the paper with one hand and cut on the line with the other hand.
- **Shoulder and trunk strength:** By placing the sheet of paper on a vertical surface, your child must lift his arm in the air and maintain that position while squeezing the eyedropper to "let it rain." To hold this position long enough to complete the activity, the shoulder girdle and trunk must be strong enough to stabilize the arm and hands.
- **Finger strength and coordination:** This activity requires strength and coordination of the thumb and first two fingers.

Note: This activity is sometimes the only way to get some children I have worked with to use a pincer grasp, particularly in the context of an art or easel-type activity. It is exciting to see a child realize that he can use his hands to create something.

> **WHY** Creating activities that have a tangible outcome for children when you are encouraging them to develop and practice fine motor skills is an excellent way to hold their interest while getting them to practice things they may perceive as difficult.

GAME ㉚ Yummy Necklace

Indoor/Outdoor

- Indoor

Equipment

- Thin elastic string (such as that used in candy necklaces)

- Blunt-end threading needle (often used for threading blocks or beads, found in art stores)
- Cereal with holes

How

- Cut a piece of string long enough to be a necklace that hangs at least 2 inches below your child's collarbone.
- Tie off one end of the string so the beads will not fall off the string.
- An adult should attach the string to the needle.
- The child pushes the needle through the cereal, pulling the string behind it.
- When the string is full of cereal, you (the adult) tie the cereal necklace together.
- Put the necklace around your child's neck, and allow her to eat the cereal.
- If you are concerned about the safety of a necklace (e.g., the child is too young) you can make a bracelet instead.
- Alternative: Use marshmallows instead of cereal; this increases the resistance but decreases the need for accuracy when threading.

Note: You may have to show the child a completed necklace (i.e., you may have to make one first).

Purpose

- **Bilateral coordination:** This requires bilateral coordination to keep the cereal still while the other hand moves the needle through the cereal.
- **In-hand manipulation:** This requires in-hand manipulation to push the needle through the cereal.
- **Eye-hand coordination:** It requires precise visual-motor control to move the needle through the hole.

> **WHY** This type of activity sets up the fingers and eyes to work together for very precise fine motor control with visual attention. Because of how much visual attention with fine motor accuracy is needed, your child is encouraged to hold the activity at a natural reading distance from the eyes (approximately 8 inches).

GAME (39) Cut 'n' Play-Doh

Indoor/Outdoor

- Either

Equipment

- Play-Doh
- Children's scissors (dull)

How

- Have your child roll the Play-Doh into a "snake," using two hands.
- The child holds the snake in one hand while cutting it with the other.
- Have the child pound the Play-Doh flat like a pizza; then you (the adult) use a pencil or knife to create outline slices in Play-Doh pizza.
- Encourage your child to cut the slices on the lines you made.

Note: If your child has difficulty manipulating the scissors to cut the snake, you can leave the Play-Doh on the flat surface and have your child put the scissors under and cut that way.

Purpose

- **Bilateral control:** This activity requires holding and stabilizing the Play-Doh, while cutting requires using both hands together.
- **In-hand manipulation:** This activity teaches how to position the hand on the scissors and how to manipulate the scissors.
- **Proprioceptive input:** Cutting against resistance increases muscle strength in the hands.

> **WHY** Teaching cutting skills in a fun way and in a three-dimensional setting prepares the child to cut on a line when in an academic setting.

GAME ④⓪ Avant-Garde Painting

Indoor/Outdoor

- Indoor

Equipment

- Small carrot sticks, corn kernels, peas, leaf from a tree, twine to use as painting utensils
- Finger paint
- Large, light-colored poster board

How

- Choose one of the larger painting utensils mentioned in Equipment (e.g., carrot sticks).
- Instruct the child to paint something you suggest (e.g., tree, person).

- Instruct the child to paint whatever interests her. If the child needs suggestions, you can tell her or show her suggested objects (e.g., geometric shapes).
- Cycle through the other painting utensils listed in Equipment, going from largest to smallest (carrot sticks to peas).

Purpose

- **Pincer grasp:** To grasp the painting utensils, especially the smaller ones, your child will need to use a pincer grasp.
- **Thumb-to-finger opposition:** Careful control of the painting utensil promotes controlled thumb-to-finger opposition.
- **Tactile input:** Touching the various utensils gives a plethora of tactile experiences.
- **Shoulder mobility:** Since this activity is done on a poster board, it encourages large drawings, which requires the painting to originate in the shoulder area.

WHY Activities that promote a functional tripod grip on a writing utensil will have lasting positive impacts for academic-type activities. Control of writing instruments can be a very difficult task for children who have sensory processing difficulties, so this activity is encouraging children to use writing-type instruments with increased success and a more mature grip on crayons, pencils, and pens that they will use in the school setting. A tripod grip consists of holding a pencil with the pad of the thumb and tip of the pointer finger, and slightly resting on the middle finger. All fingers are bent with even pressure distributed among the three fingers. A tripod grip allows the child to write more quickly and easily while decreasing fatigue to the hand and wrist.

GAME (41) Grab a Piece of the Action

. . . . .

Indoor/Outdoor

- Indoor

Equipment

- Any or all of the following: beanbags, squishy balls of various sizes, stuffed animals, all about fist-sized or smaller
- Small cars that wind up or pull back and go
- Dull tongs, barbeque type
- Bag that will hold the items
- Bouncy ball with handle (sufficient for your child to sit on)

How

- Lay the items out on the floor, and have the child pick them up with the tongs and put them in the bag.
- Next place the items under and on top of various places throughout the house. The child picks them up using the tongs.
- Have the child chase the small car around the room, and let her "win" if she can pick it up with the tongs before it stops.
- Another option is to have the child try to pick up objects off the floor using the tongs while bouncing or lying on the bouncy ball with the items spread out in front of her.

Purpose

- **Fine motor skills:** This activity develops strength in the hand as well as fine motor skills.
- **Bilateral coordination:** Grasping the bag in one hand and stuffing objects into the bag with the other hand develops bilateral coordination.

■ **Visual skills:** Some objects are stationary and others moving; the child must move to get them, so it promotes eye pursuits and saccades as well as steady fixation on the object. Eye pursuits are the smooth tracking movements of your eyes that allow them to follow a moving target. Saccades are quick eye movements that allow your eyes to quickly scan a large area.

■ **Eye-hand coordination:** The motor response to visual input, both fixed and moving, challenges the eyes and hands to work together to grasp the items.

WHY Integration of the fine motor skills with the basic body sensory components (tactile, proprioceptive) as well as the visual and gross motor system will challenge your child in a multisensory fashion, but due to the fun nature of the activity, your child is less likely to become frustrated.

5

COMMUNICATION

WE KNOW THE brain is primed for language at birth because studies of newborns' brains show electrical brain energy increases in the left hemisphere when a child hears language. When you talk to your infant, you provide the child with more than words. Your facial expressions teach that words are linked to different expressions, and your tone teaches differences in emotion hidden in words. You provide the child with a basis for intonation, which stimulates the brain.

Using language is one of the most intricate sensorimotor tasks the brain-and-body team must carry out. It involves virtually all of the sensory nervous system and is the most complex task for your motor planning (praxis) system. To engage in conversation you must hear the words around you. The ear is designed to grab sound, which engages the auditory processing system, stimulating the auditory cortex where the sound is processed. Once the brain recognizes the sounds as words, the signal is sent down the language pathways to associate the words with meanings. The brain automatically scrolls through its built-in dictionary to find the words. To give the words their true meaning, it looks for the semantic meaning of the word (i.e., straight definition) and then how the word was used in the sentence. The brain then attaches associated concepts. Finally, the last task is to consider the pragmatics (i.e., social context of a word's usage) attached to the words.

Comprehending language is a process that attaches meaning to a code. Once the brain understands the words being used, the conceptual system located throughout the brain attaches associations and higher-order thinking to the words. It does this by searching pathways that have been formed from past experiences. The brain sends signals down these experiential pathways to comprehend what has been heard. This comprehension allows the brain to form an appropriate response to what has been heard.

The important point to consider is that comprehension involves understanding not the literal meanings of the words and phrases but rather the intended or conveyed meanings. Listeners use their knowledge of the world, the speaker, social parameters, and the particular situation to comprehend.

Now the challenge for the brain is to hunt for the words to formulate a response. The brain taps the conceptual system to meet the challenge. The brain works on forming the words into ideas and making sure the ideas are put into a construct called grammar so others can comprehend the concept. Last, the words are given intonation to express appropriate emphasis, emotion, and intent.

This sequence gives you a sense of how involved this motor process is for speaking. For us to say words, the brain must physically make the words and concepts happen. It electrically signals the larynx, throat, tongue, lips, and facial muscles to produce the correct sounds. Sound is created when these parts of the body make the air vibrate. The intent is to have those within a close space having their auditory systems.

Language is multidimensional and involves a variety of integrated skills that require cognition and linguistic knowledge. Opportunities to perform language and an environment that reinforces communication are crucial since difficulties with processing language (language disorders) do not exist in the language but rather in the child. The activities and games in this chapter and throughout this book place an emphasis on the child and offer a variety of situations that elicit language responses. All interactions where a child conveys his or her thoughts to another human being are language and should be encouraged or rewarded. In the language games, you invite the child to relate aspects of his or her shared environment to another person, soliciting joint attention and connectedness.

It is language that makes speech meaningful!

GAME ㊷ Peek-a-Boo

Equipment

- A small towel

How

- Hide your face behind the towel, and then show yourself and say "Boo!"
- Wait for child's response—a slight change in facial expression or a laugh—then repeat immediately when you get any reaction from the child; this will reinforce any communication and increase his desire to communicate.
- Alternative: Try covering your face with a small towel and while under it say, "Peeka," and wait a few seconds and then say,

---

"Boo," while pulling the towel off your face. Continue doing this and continue waiting before pulling the towel off to see if your child will verbally "jump in" and say, "Boo."

Purpose

■ **Understanding of early object concepts:** Object permanence is the concept that objects continue to exist while they are out of sight.

■ **Joint attention:** This simple activity uses the element of surprise to entice early joint attention.

■ **Social interaction:** Responding to a caregiver's facial expression is one of the early skills of social reciprocity.

> **WHY** Research has indicated that the concept of object permanence is a necessary development for the emergence of first words.

GAME ㊸ Red Light, Green Light

Indoor/Outdoor

■ Indoor

Equipment

■ Two pieces of construction paper (one red, one green)
■ Hippity Hop ball (This old-fashioned toy revived from the seventies is a large ball with a handle on it, which kids sit on

to bounce forward. You can purchase these at most toy stores.)

How

- First teach your child that green means "Go" and red means "Stop."
- Have someone else hold the red or green paper up; let child know that green is for *go* and red is for *stop*.
- You will hold your child's hand and move or stop with the child. While moving, continually say, "Green light." Overexaggerate the stopping motion and say, "Red light." Most children will get this quickly because you are linking movement with colors and words.
- Introduce the Hippity Hop, and stand several feet in front of the child. Alternate holding up the red paper to indicate "stop" or green paper to indicate "go." You may also need to say, "Stop" and "Go" to link verbal cues with the visual cues.

How (Including Peers)

- Choose a caller to be the person in charge of saying "Green light" and "Red light" and holding up the paper.
- Line up all the participants 10 to 20 feet from the caller.
- When the caller says, "Green light," everyone hops toward the caller until he says, "Red light." At "Red light," the participants must stop moving.
- The person who maneuvers closest to the caller gets to be the caller in the next round.
- Alternative: This game can be done by crawling or hopping for younger children. This game can also be done outside using tricycles.

Note: I and a speech therapist worked with three boys to get them "ready" for this activity. First we made sure each boy understood the difference between red and green and could identify the colors from other colors. Then we taught each boy the stop/go concept associated with red and green by physically motoring him through the action. One of us held the boy's hand while the other held up the green colored paper and yelled "Go!" The one who continued to hold the boy's hand reiterated "Go!" and moved with him until the red (stop) sign was held up. Then we taught the concept again, this time saying "Red light!" and "Green light!"

We first tried the game without the Hippity Hop balls, but two of the boys had a hard time stopping from running, even when the red light was shown. So we introduced the Hippity Hop balls, and we noticed that all three boys paid increased attention to the caller and were better able to control their bodies. This is probably due to the proprioceptive input received by bouncing on the Hippity Hop balls. We filmed the activity, and it was so fun to watch all three of these five-year-old boys with autism engaged to the point of belly laughing.

Purpose

- **Body control:** Using the Hippity Hop ball helps children increase stop/start control over their bodies.
- **Environmental cues:** All participants learn to follow auditory and visual cues.
- **Language concepts:** This game encourages basic language concepts linked with visual cues for those concepts. It also helps foster paying attention to another speaker and following directions.
- **Preacademic skills:** Pairing movement with the colors increases a child's understanding of the concept that green means "go" and red means "stop."
- **Proprioception:** Hopping, as well as stop/start motion, gives increased input to the joints.

- **Social interaction:** This is a good game to encourage your child to participate with a peer since it is a sensorimotor activity with a clear goal that requires minimal interaction but mutual enjoyment.

> **WHY** Ninety percent of the earliest verbs are learned while the action is taking place. By linking language and movement, we strengthen language acquisition.

GAME (44) Working Memory

Indoor/Outdoor

- Indoor

Equipment

- Duplicate picture cards of the following: common actions (e.g., jumping), common objects (e.g., car), places (e.g., house), descriptive concepts (e.g., tall, under, behind); created by taking pictures of common items in the child's world
- Poster board with a 4-inch-by-4-inch grid drawn on it

How

- Start off with two pairs of cards, working up to six or seven pairs of cards as the child's skill increases.
- Place them facedown in the grid boxes on the poster board in front of the child. Creating a visual grid helps keep the cards in place and aids the child to create a visual schema.

- Explain the rules of the game.
- The child is going to be a detective and find the two duplicate cards. If the child picks cards that do not match, then she should put them back down exactly where she found them and try to remember their locations—it might help her later. When she finds two that are the same, she needs to make a sentence using the word on the cards (e.g., house: "I live in a big house."). Then she puts the cards in her pile.
- Then you take a turn.

Purpose

- **Working memory:** By remembering where the cards are placed, your child enhances his or her working memory. To allow a time lapse that reinforces the working memory, always be sure to take a turn after your child.
- **Rule following:** Your child works on following the rules of a simple game.
- **Turn taking:** This tabletop activity works on turn taking.
- **Language:** Since the pictures are things in your child's environment, they will help elicit language. Also, by talking about each picture briefly, you provide more information about the picture and thus give more for your child's memory to grasp when he or she searches for the picture again.

WHY Many children with autism struggle with their working memory, which is an essential part of conversational language. Typical games that work on this issue use pictures of objects, animals, or places that may or may not be in the child's world. So they may not have a connection to these items. Creating a game that incorporates familiar items to develop the child's working memory will be fruitful.

GAME ㊺ Where in My World

Indoor/Outdoor

- Either

Equipment

- Any high-interest item (sensory ball, stuffed animal, windup toy, car)
- A cup
- Preferred snack

How

- Place the item *in, on, next to, under,* or *behind* the cup, introducing prepositions.
- Ask the child where the item is located.
- Initially give the child a choice (e.g., *under* or *over*); then have the child answer a where question.
- If the child is able to correctly describe where the favorite item is using a single word (e.g., *over*) or prepositional phrase (e.g., "The fish is behind the cup."), then the child gets to eat the snack or play with the high-interest item.

Purpose

- **Language concepts:** This game incorporates some basic prepositional concepts such as *over, behind, under,* and so on.
- **Language concepts:** This activity promotes answering and asking *where* questions.
- **Utterance length:** Responses can range from one-word answers to longer utterances where you can model as much or as little detail as necessary.

GAME ㊻ Character Commands

Indoor/Outdoor

- Indoor

Equipment

- Picture of your child's favorite character (e.g., SpongeBob, Thomas the Tank)
- Wooden craft stick

How

- This is a takeoff on the game Simon Says that uses the character as the director of actions.
- Paste the picture of the chosen character on to end of wooden craft stick.
- Tell the child that you are going to play a game and SpongeBob (or Thomas, Dora, Flash Gordon, etc.) will tell the child exactly what to do. Tell the child to do only what the character says to do.

Note: If you know it will be too frustrating to go back and forth between you and the character giving instructions, have only SpongeBob give the instructions. This is especially true for young children or those with receptive language difficulties. Remember, the main goal is getting the child to follow a verbal direction.

- Let the child know to listen carefully, since SpongeBob will try to trick the child.
- After the direction is followed, ask the child to tell you what he or she did.
- Once your child is used to SpongeBob as the director of actions, SpongeBob can be used to elicit cooperation throughout daily activities by having him request that the child "pick up his clothes," and so on.

Purpose

- **Following directions:** This activity teaches kids to follow verbal directions using auditory input.
- **Listening skills:** To carry out the activity, your child must pay attention to what the character is saying.
- **Language comprehension:** This activity helps with understanding action words and one- to two-step commands.

WHY Most children with autism or Asperger's syndrome are strong visual learners who struggle with auditory memory. This game provides a nonconsequential way for your child to practice auditory memory. During their primary grades in school, children are given many visual cues, that is, directions on the board, or date and time of events displayed. This begins to change around the third grade because teachers begin expecting children to follow and remember auditory information, and they provide fewer visual cues.

GAME (47) Prepositions and Me

....

Indoor/Outdoor

■ Either

Equipment

■ 4-inch-by-5-inch index cards
■ Possibly pictures

How

■ For children who cannot read: make index cards depicting prepositions (*on, under,* etc.) by using downloaded pictures from the Internet.

■ For children who can read: make index cards with prepositions (*on, under,* etc.) written on them.

■ Have the child pick a card and act out the picture or word. For example, have the child show you what *under* means by crawling under a table. Or the child can demonstrate "on the chair" or "beside the stove."

■ If your child has difficulty understanding how this game works, show the child by picking a card and saying, "on the chair: Mommy is sitting on the chair."

Purpose

■ **Language development:** This activity provides a way to teach prepositions through actions. It is exciting to hear children use prepositions correctly once they experience the concept themselves. Once your child has played this game several times and starts to get these concepts, help the child generalize the knowledge further: give the child directions that include prepositional concepts about how to find things or what the child needs to do, and see if the child can follow them.

> **WHY** Children with neurological difficulties often have difficulty conceptualizing prepositions. It is possible to make a child memorize the word *under* by showing the child a word paired with a picture of "under a bed" over and over again. Sometimes when children learn these concepts in a two-dimensional manner (on paper or computer) they do not internalize these kinds of concepts. So when they see the word during reading, it does not translate automatically to their understanding of spatial concepts in their environment, which impacts their reading comprehension.

GAME ㊽ What's Missing?

Indoor/Outdoor

- Indoor

Equipment

- A swing or a large exercise ball

How

- Swing your child on a swing to the rhythm of a familiar song or rhyme, such as, "Row, Row, Row Your Boat Gently Down the Stream," several times.
- Then swing the child and leave off the ending. For example, leave off the word *stream,* and wait for your child to finish the song or rhythm for you.

- You can do the same thing with rhymes.
- If you don't have access to a swing, use a ball. Bounce your child to the rhythm of a familiar rhyme, such as, "Humpty Dumpty sat on a wall, Humpty Dumpty had a great fall."
- Again leave off the last word after you have done this several times.
- Then move on to more songs and more rhymes.

Purpose

- **Language:** This activity is designed to elicit language in children who are less verbal or who have difficulty being spontaneously verbal.
- **Auditory memory:** Rhythm and rhyme of familiar songs lay pathways in the brain, increasing memory of the words.
- **Vestibular input:** Swinging and bouncing both engage the vestibular system, which is intertwined with the auditory system.

Note: A three-and-a-half-year-old boy who was nonverbal, except for some yelling utterances, and exhibited almost no eye contact inadvertently taught this game to me many years ago. I was swinging him and singing, "Row, Row, Row Your Boat," to calm him at the beginning of a therapy session. He looked at me, held my gaze, and said a word that sounded like "merry," and then looked away. I kept singing, looking at him intently, and he kept looking at me. Then I intentionally left off the word "stream," and he uttered something that sounded like "stream." After several therapy sessions, he was clearly finishing the words in the song. I asked his mom to stay in the room for a session, and she was amazed. We both fought back tears, but we continued to use this as a strategy to elicit language, of course using different songs and introducing new words.

WHY The vestibular and auditory systems are directly linked. The two systems are connected both anatomically and physiologically, as both are located in the inner ear and even share some nerve fibers. When we hear sounds, the gravity receptors in the ear are stimulated and the vestibular system responds. Therefore, there is a direct link between movement and sound. There is also evidence that stimulating the vestibular system can elicit spontaneous vocalizations. Spontaneous vocalizations begin in infancy and are a prerequisite for functional language communication.

GAME ㊼ **How Does It End?**

Indoor/Outdoor

■ Either

Equipment

■ Short books with simple story lines. The best ones are traditional fairy tales such as *Three Little Pigs, Hansel and Gretel, Jack and the Beanstalk,* and *Goldilocks and the Three Bears.)*

How (First Level)

■ Read or tell your child a story that he has heard several times, but this time stop before you get to the ending. Ask your child to tell you how it ends. Say, "How does it end?"

Note: Try to avoid saying, "Can you tell me?" or "Do you remember . . . how it ends." Because the child may say, "Nope, I can't," and you enter a bargaining game instead of a learning activity.

- Many children will formulate answers. If your child is struggling with this, provide him with a few verbal prompts, such as, "What happened to the wolf?"
- This can be a very difficult activity for children with a spectrum diagnosis, so make sure to keep it light and fun, even if you have to be the one creating the new endings until your child starts to interject.

How (Second Level)

- Read a simple story to your child, but stop before you read the ending. Then ask your child how the story *could* end, the idea is to try to get your child to discuss different ways it could end.
- If your child has already heard the story, he may have a difficult time mentally moving away from the ending he already knows. So you may need to find a book or make up a simple story he has not heard before.

Note: For older children you can use familiar movies. Talk through the movie events and then discuss ways it could have ended differently.

Purpose

- **Auditory memory:** This activity works on auditory memory skills.
- **Imagination:** This game promotes imagination and basic storytelling by using a familiar story as a "jumping off" point for your child.
- **Executive function:** This activity teaches that there is not always one way to solve a problem and that there can be different solutions.
- **Theory of mind:** To think of "new" endings for stories, children have to try to think like the character. This may be very difficult,

but it steers children toward trying to understand the thoughts of others.

Note: I recently used this activity when working with a fourth grader with a diagnosis of Asperger's. He was a good reader but really had a hard time with fictional books, preferring nonfiction (just the facts) books, which is not unusual for children with autism, Asperger's, or sensory processing disorder. When we first started playing the game, he didn't like it and really struggled with ideas. But after a few times, he started to come up with creative "new endings" for books and also started to understand why people write books that are not about "actual" things, events, or people.

WHY Children with autism and Asperger's can be rigid in their understanding and view of the world. They are sometimes perfectionists who want games and activities to go a special way and not to veer from their idea of how it "should be done." This activity allows them to realize that there is often more than one way to do an activity.

GAME ⑤⓪ In One Ear and Out the Other!

Indoor/Outdoor
- Either

Equipment
- Mr. Potato Head
- Felt board or whiteboard with marker

How

- The adult physically manipulates Mr. Potato Head to illustrate certain idioms. Act out the intended meaning of the idiom while physically showing the literal meaning with Mr. Potato Head's body.
- Suggested idioms include "It goes in one ear and out the other," "I'm all ears," "Your eyes are bigger than your stomach," "You took the words right out of my mouth," "You're pulling my leg," "Hats off to you!" and "I smell something brewing."

Purpose

- **Language concepts:** By physically moving Mr. Potato Head, you can illustrate the idiom literally and show how fun and silly idioms can be.
- **Language understanding:** This activity is designed to show that words and phrases are not always literal.

WHY Children with autism or Asperger's often struggle with pragmatic language. Difficulty with pragmatic language impacts a child's friendship-making skills, affects the understanding of humor and sarcasm, and can affect reading comprehension. This activity provides a concrete way to work on an aspect of pragmatic language by showing the child how words don't always mean the same thing. Metaphors require a person to understand the implied meaning of a word or phrase rather than the literal meaning. Examples of metaphors include, "My memory of the party is a bit foggy," or "My dad was boiling mad."

GAME ⑤ Order in the House!

Indoor/Outdoor

- Indoor

Equipment

- Sequence cards of everyday home activities (available at an educational school supply store), such as getting dressed, brushing teeth, making a sandwich (You can also make your own by taking pictures with your digital camera.)

How

- First, show the child all the cards in a particular sequence.
- Then place four sequence cards facedown in front of you. Have the child pick up a card and describe what is happening.
- Ask the child if this is the first event that occurs in the sequence: "Is this the first thing to happen?" If not, the child has to put it back down and pick another card.

Purpose

- **Sequencing skills:** This activity provides an opportunity to reinforce early sequence skills by doing and talking about everyday activities.
- **Visual memory:** This activity plays off a strength for many children—visual attention—while challenging their understanding of sequential organization.
- **Activities of daily living:** This activity provides a framework for children to organize and sequence activities they do daily, therefore speeding up the process when they engage in an activity such as getting dressed.

WHY Because of the executive function impairments in children with autism, Asperger's, or other neurological diagnoses, they have difficulty with sequencing tasks. Leveraging a regiment the child is familiar with reinforces sequencing skills and language.

6

SOCIAL SENSE

Social sense is truly a sense, and it requires the automaticity of a well-integrated sensory system, *theory of mind* capabilities, as well as a cognitive grasp of social situations. It is probably the first "extra-person" sense. Theory of mind is the awareness of one's mental states such as beliefs, desires, intents, and knowledge, as well as the awareness that others have such states, which may be different from one's own. It allows us to understand that someone else may have needs different from ours, and it is essential for empathy.

The development of our social sense begins early, perhaps before we are born. Brain research confirms that our brains are wired in a way that drives us to connect with those around us. In the beginning, our sensory-nervous systems drive our connections to those around us. We connect to the sound of our mother's voice beginning in utero, we are soothed to sleep by the touch and rocking of another, and before we can speak, we learn to read the actions of another who is meeting our needs.

Early social sense is seen in infants when they react to the facial expression of an adult—when they first begin to realize that their smile or babbling elicits a reaction from those around them. One of the early stages of social sense is joint attention, following the gaze of another, or using eye contact and gestures as a way to garner and direct the attention of those around them. For instance, if an infant is interested in an Elmo doll on the counter, then he or she will stare at it and maybe pair the visual direction with a gesture toward it as a way of communicating to the caregiver that the infant wants the Elmo doll. Infants will start to display joint attention as early as six months old, and it is usually fully developed by twelve months of life. Many researchers believe that early joint attention is the basis for social cognition. Lack of joint attention impedes us from sharing similar emotional reactions to events, that is, to things going on around us as well as things we observe in our environment.

Children become more refined in their social sense with the development of theory of mind, which is the ability to understand the needs and wants of others without them being made explicit: for example, when a child realizes his sister would not be interested in getting a Batman figure for Christmas and would prefer a Hannah Montana doll. Another way to think about theory of mind is that it is a concept that assumes that other people have their own thoughts and feelings that may differ from our own. In essence, they have a mind of their own, hence the term *theory of mind*. We can start to see theory of mind begin to develop between the ages of three and four. (But remember I said *begin*.) Impairment of theory of mind development has direct impact on development of empathetic drive, intuitive social understanding, pragmatic language, as well as some academic skills such as reading comprehension. For example, say you cannot wait to tell your friend that you got a new PlayStation. But before you can tell her the good news, she tells you that her puppy got hit by a car this week. Theory of mind allows you to understand that this is not the proper time to share your information, because your friend is sad.

Teaching children components of social skills and helping them understand how their sensory nervous system guides them in social interaction are key to helping them develop a social sense. The games in this chapter encourage a number of objectives, all of which lead to greater social sense. These objectives include paying more attention to and interacting with those around the child and learning to recognize little things, such as a downturned mouth, which means someone might be sad. This gives insight into how to navigate a social situation.

Although social cognition is intertwined with the development of the nervous system, and children with neurological difficulties such as autism usually show impaired social cognition and display a lack of social drive, there are certain social sense skills that can be taught that will help children understand how to make social connections thus helping develop their social sense.

GAME (52) Tickle Game

■■

Indoor/Outdoor

- Indoor

Equipment

- None

How

- Start with gentle tickling. Be careful not to tickle beyond the point where it is enjoyable to the child.

- On occasion, stop until the child asks you to start again.
- If your child seems fearful of this type of interaction, you can demonstrate by tickling a doll and making the doll laugh so that your child understands that the interaction is fun.
- Show your child how to tickle you, too. Laugh hard, and give lots of eye contact.
- Stop when requested—develop a physical signal for "stop." Suggest using the basic sign for "stop," which is putting a hand up.

Note: For children who are averse to light touch (tactilely defensive), try the following Rowboat Game:

- Sit with your legs forward in a V.
- Place your child facing you with his legs pressed against your legs.
- Grasp your child's elbows firmly, and rock back and forth while looking at the child.
- Sing "Rocking Mommy, rocking Tommy" and repeat. (Use your name or title if you are not the mother.)
- Stop after a while, and wait for the child to request that you start again.

Purpose

- **Social reciprocity:** By encouraging your child to tickle you back or pull back during the rowboat game, you are teaching social tit for tat.
- **Eye contact:** The nature of the Tickle Game or Rowboat Game is that you are facing each other and sharing a common experience, which promotes eye contact.
- **Joint attention:** The common experience, especially while facing each other, coaxes your child toward joint attention.

> **WHY** This shared experience uses one of the most basic senses (touch—both light and deep) to promote joint attention and then social reciprocity, encouraging human bonding.

GAME ㊼ Face Missing

Indoor/Outdoor

- Indoor

Equipment

- Whiteboard and whiteboard pens

How (First Level)

- Draw faces showing various emotions on a whiteboard.
- Have the child identify the emotion being depicted.
- As the child advances, use less detail when showing the various emotions so as to prompt the child to look for clues with less information.

How (Second Level)

- Draw a face, erase part of it, and have your child fill in the missing parts based on the emotion you describe.

Purpose

- **Emotional recognition:** This game helps with facial recognition as well as attaching emotional meaning to facial expressions.
- **Visual memory:** As the game advances, children have to remember what part of the face is missing.

- **Gestalt:** This game encourages children to attend to the whole picture, not simply the parts of a picture.

> **WHY** The way we garner information about people's internal states is by understanding the nuances of facial and body language. Autistic children tend to have difficulty picking up on the cues that people give when displaying subtle emotions, so they can appear insensitive to others when they are not responding as others would expect. By creating fun games to familiarize children with the meaning of facial expressions, we help them in a concrete, visual way to recognize how a person might feel or what might be happening to make a person feel in different ways and give them an opportunity to talk about it. Research has shown that people with autism do exhibit the same neural motor responses in the brain as others. It is crucial to create fun games that familiarize children with the meaning of certain facial expressions.

GAME 54 Guess Who?

Indoor/Outdoor

- Indoor

Equipment

- Digital camera
- Printer
- Photo paper
- Scissors

How

- Take close-up pictures of family members' faces and your child's, and print the pictures on sturdy photo card stock, or have photos prepared at traditional photo processing establishment.
- Then cut the photos into large pieces; make sure each piece contains a distinguishable part of the face: for example, an eye, mouth, and so on. Start out simple: cut only two large squares from each face; then lay out the faces with the missing pieces in front of the child.
- Place the pieces upside down in a pile.
- Have the child pick one piece, look at it, and try to guess whose face it belongs to. Then you take a turn and draw a card. Repeat until all the faces are guessed.
- Start out with only two faces, and then keep adding more as your child understands the game and begins to learn to identify the faces.
- Then put the missing pieces into a pile, and have the child draw a card and match it to the face with that part missing.

Purpose

- **Facial recognition:** This activity encourages children to attend to facial features of familiar faces.
- **Visual memory:** There is quite a bit of documentation that children with autism do not attend to the faces of others. This game encourages that sort of observation in a fun way.

> **WHY** Research has shown that children with autism or Asperger's do not register the faces of the people around them in the same way as others. Imaging studies, positron emission tomography (PET), and functional magnetic resonance imaging (FMRI) indicate that the brains of individuals with autism fail to recruit brain regions specialized for faces. This game helps increase your child's awareness of the faces of the people in your child's world in a concrete manner.

GAME ⑤ Ping-Pong Compliment Game

Indoor/Outdoor

- Indoor

Equipment

- A large bag of white Ping-Pong balls
- Large, clear jar

How

- Each time your child gives a compliment, write it on a ball and put it into the large, clear jar.
- When the jar is full, decide how you are going to celebrate—preferably with a friend.

Purpose

- **Spontaneous social interaction:** Giving compliments spontaneously is the next step for children who are learning new social rules, and it is a very difficult task to master, so this game provides an instant visual reward.
- **Visual reminder:** Placed in a visible place in the house, the jar continually serves as a reminder to the child and puts the act of complimenting "on his agenda."
- **Learning a reward system:** This game is ongoing and teaches children short- and long-term rewards.

> **WHY** The Ping-Pong Compliment Game is a way to reward the newly learned behavior and to continue promoting spontaneously social interaction. I love what happens in a child's world when he learns the power of observing and then complimenting others, because the reaction starts a self-reinforcing cycle in which others start complimenting the child back.

GAME 56 Pointing Fun

Indoor/Outdoor

- Indoor

Equipment

- Clear plastic bag
- Small edibles such as candy, cookies
- Small objects (crayon, penny, straw, block, key, etc.)

How (First Level)

- Place items in a clear bag, and encourage the child to point at something she wants. At first utilize only one type of item, cookie, or candy.
- Once she points, you overexaggerate the pointing motion and say, "Good pointing, you want . . . something." Immediate verbal response to the pointing is key to this game.
- Repeat the process.

Note: If your child is having difficulty pointing, you will need to use hand-over-hand assistance by taking her pointer finger and placing it on top of the item in the bag that you know or think the child wants. This is one reason using something edible is a good way to start this game, because you know your child will prefer that above other items. Once you have shown your child physically, respond to the "prompted" gesture by saying, "You want the cookie," and giving it to the child.

How (Second Level)

■ Put different items in the bag (include food your child likes) to encourage visual discrimination and to make sure the child is not simply pointing at anything randomly.

■ Usually an edible treat will be the favorite.

How (Third Level)

■ As your child begins to understand this game, increase the visual space that the child must scan as well as the number of items to choose from.

■ Use a table a few feet away with more items in the bag. Then use a table across the room.

Purpose

■ **Joint attention:** This activity teaches your child to facilitate joint attention between you and your child.

■ **Pointing:** This activity reinforces isolation of the pointer finger.

■ **Visual scanning:** By beginning with a small plastic bag, the child learns to visually scan a small, contained space and fixate on what he wants and then to do the same with a larger space.

■ **Visual discrimination:** This activity teaches a child how to visually discriminate items that are close together and locate the item he wants. It gives opportunities for a child to learn to discriminate foreground from background information.

WHY Joint attention is one of the early social reference skills that people learn as a way to bring those around them into their world. Pointing is a component of joint attention, and many children who struggle later in life with social skills lacked early social reference skills such as pointing. However, it is a skill we can teach, and by teaching the skill of pointing we help a child communicate with us. Once a child learns the power of pointing and starts using this tool, the child opens up a whole new way of sharing his world. It profoundly changes the association with those around that child. For me, a parent following the pointing finger of his or her child and connecting with what the child is communicating is one of the most moving things a person can witness, "Yes, yes, you want your bear!"

GAME ⑤⑦ People Bingo

Indoor/Outdoor

- Either

Equipment

- Draw grids with either four boxes (2 by 2) or nine boxes (3 by 3); create bingo cards by putting names of family or friends in each of the boxes (pictures for nonreaders).
- Small pieces of paper to make cards with one description on each: include physical traits (e.g., brown hair), things people like (e.g., pizza, fishing), professions (e.g., teacher), and state of residence (e.g., Texas)

How

- Take turns with your child drawing a card from the pile of papers with descriptions.
- Match the card to the people on the bingo cards.
- The goal is to fill up the bingo card with the characteristics that match the people on the bingo card.

Purpose

- **Observational skills:** This activity challenges children to pay attention to people's physical traits.
- **Theory of mind:** This game helps children understand that others have likes and dislikes that differ from their own. It is a pre-theory-of-mind skill.
- **Conversational language:** Knowing key things that others like and dislike as well as information about others, such as professions, gives children fodder for beginning conversations.

Note: The parents of a boy I have worked with said that after they played this game several times, their son started to ask relatives questions about themselves and would insist on creating more cards. Both parents said that he had never seemed interested in others, but after making the qualities of family members and friends a game, he was suddenly motivated. The great thing about it was that his asking questions of family members resulted in their starting to ask him questions and talk to him more.

WHY By using physical traits, the activity plays on the objective observations (e.g., hair color). You can expand it to subjective observations such as likes and dislikes (e.g., likes pizza, dislikes cats). This game will give the child a reason to have an interest in other people and understand that although different, everyone can share common interests, hobbies, and traits.

GAME (58) My Brain, Your Brain

Indoor/Outdoor

- Indoor

Equipment

- Age-appropriate books or magazines
- Small whiteboard for each player
- Whiteboard markers

How (First Level)

- Players take turns flipping to different pages in a book or magazine.
- Then silently and without the other player seeing, each has to write down what the picture on the page makes him or her think about.
- Each player needs to write one word that best describes the first thing that pops into his or her mind.
- Then they compare the words on their boards and discuss what they wrote and why.

Note: Once your child understands how to play this game, it is best played with two children. However, you and your child can play it together when she is learning the game.

How (Second Level)

- You can make it more challenging by having both participants write down the word they think their friend is going to write.
- If you have a larger group of children, pick one child to write down what he or she thinks when seeing the picture.

- The other children in the group try to guess what the chosen student is going to write down.

Note: This game may require an adult prompter to facilitate conversation about what each child was thinking when he or she saw the picture.

- Alternative: For younger children, let them draw a picture of what is in their mind.

Purpose

- **Theory of mind:** It is an excellent way for children of every age to figure out that others can see the same thing but think about something different.
- **Executive function:** Generating one word from a picture helps children organize thoughts and decide on one under a time limit.
- **Social interaction:** This activity involves interacting with others with a specific purpose for the interaction.

> **WHY** Theory of mind is the ability to understand that others have a "mind of their own." It is the comprehension that other people have wants and desires, likes and dislikes that may differ from our own. This activity reinforces the idea of theory of mind by forcing the child to think beyond him- or herself about what others experience and think.

■■■

Indoor/Outdoor

■ Indoor

Equipment

■ A clear acrylic children's easel
■ Shaving cream

How

■ You stand on one side of the acrylic easel, and your child stands on the other side of the easel.
■ Put a few dollops of shaving cream on both sides of the easel.
■ Start by making large, overexaggerated strokes as you spread the shaving cream.
■ Once your child starts spreading the shaving cream, start mimicking the child's strokes.
■ Make sure to keep your face close to the easel so your child can easily see your facial expression and that you are having fun.
■ Alternative: If your child is tactilly defensive, let the child use a sponge to make the strokes with the shaving cream. The sponge should be soft but dry and about the size of your child's palm. Another way to play this game is to cover both sides of the acrylic easel with shaving cream.

Note: A colleague of mine uses this activity when she goes into homes to work with children who have autism. She does it to establish a fun relationship as well as to show parents how something seemingly nonpurposeful can do so much for the child. It also gives the parent who wants to interact with the child an easy, fun activity to do so.

Purpose

- **Motor imitation skills:** We first learn imitation through simple motor responsibilities.
- **Contingent imitation:** By imitating the child's strokes, you teach the child how to imitate.
- **Tactile input:** Shaving cream is a longtime favorite of occupational therapists when working on tactile processing.
- **Social interaction:** This is a joint activity because you are working in unison, but it is less demanding for children because there is an easel between you and your child.

Note: Once your child can do this with you, it is a great activity to have the child play with a peer.

> **WHY** Early imitation is the key to learning for all children. Children who struggle neurologically may have difficulty with this early skill; thus, activities that promote imitation lay the foundation for children to learn through imitation.

GAME ⑥⓪ Body Pointing

Indoor/Outdoor

- Either

Equipment

- Names of body parts written on strips of paper: *finger, nose, chin, eyes, knees, head, shoulder, elbow, foot, hip*
- Hat or bowl

How

■ Fold the strips of paper and put them in a hat or bowl.

■ Have the child pick out a strip of paper. Then have her point to some object in the room, using the body part indicated on the paper.

■ The other participants in the game must guess what the person is pointing at.

Note: This is an advanced game that is best done with children eight years old or older and who have some language skills. I have watched children who were in a group doing this activity move from being seemingly uncomfortable and almost rigid in their movements to being relaxed, laughing, and appearing amazed that others can guess what they are pointing at.

Purpose

■ **Body language:** This activity teaches children to communicate with their body and without words.

■ **Joint attention:** This activity teaches advanced joint attention skills without the pressure of language.

> **WHY** The ability to communicate via body language is an essential social skill; it often makes the difference between effective and noneffective communicators. Children with neurological processing difficulties may learn the words to express themselves, but they often struggle with effective nonverbal body communication skills.

GAME (61) Emotional Potato Head

Indoor/Outdoor

- Indoor

Equipment

- Mr. Potato Head Silly Suitcase
- Any other Mr. Potato Head accessories you can get your hands on, especially different mouths and eyes
- Deck of cards with pictures of facial emotions (You can also make these cards yourself; if your child is at reading level, write different emotions on notecards.)

How

- The way to approach this is to build Mr. Potato Head purposefully.
- Have the child choose a card with an emotion that can be made with the Mr. Potato Head parts on hand.
- Have the child try to duplicate the emotion on Mr. Potato Head.
- Talk about how Mr Potato Head is feeling and why he may be feeling this way.

Purpose

- **Empathetic registration:** This activity allows children to learn to read emotions in others "outside themselves."
- **Empathetic duplications:** It also allows children to learn to duplicate the emotions of others; it reinforces the registration of emotions.

- **Theory of mind:** For higher-functioning children on the spectrum, you can use Mr. Potato Head to elicit a conversation about what he (Mr. Potato Head) is thinking.
- **Fine motor skills:** Manipulating the components to construct Mr. Potato Head promotes fine motor skills.
- **Language expansion:** By having the child tell you what Mr Potato Head is feeling, you are eliciting descriptive language.

> **WHY** When children do not register and understand the facial expressions of others, it is impossible for them to ascribe meaning to these expressions. This activity is a nonthreatening way to learn that a downward smile means someone is sad or raised eyebrows mean that someone is surprised.

GAME (62) Don't Drop the Ball

Indoor/Outdoor

- Either

Equipment

- Tactile ball, Koosh ball, or oversized Hacky Sack (A Koosh ball is available at most toy stores and is easy to purchase on the Internet.)

How

- Have the child place the ball on her head.
- You (the adult) make faces at the child, who then attempts to mimic the faces.

- While attempting to mimic the faces, your child should attempt to balance the ball on her head.

Purpose

- **Balance:** Keeping the ball balanced during the mimicking exercise requires the child's additional attention to her body while conducting this activity.
- **Human interaction and social development:** In this activity, the child attempts to recognize and mimic facial expressions, which requires attention to others.
- **Split attention:** This activity requires attention to two disparate tasks.

> **WHY** Thus far, many of the activities in this book have used a two-dimensional medium to get children to attend to facial expressions. Then they used three-dimensional items to replicate facial expressions, such as a Mr. Potato Head. This activity brings it to the next level by getting the child to attend to another person's face while balancing a ball at the same time. The ball adds a sensory input to the cranial area, which has an alerted effect that helps with concentration. Your child will simply see it as fun.

7

SCHOOL READY

BUILDING ON SENSORIMOTOR or language skills introduced in the previous chapters, this chapter hones in on the specific preacademic and academic concepts that will be intertwined throughout your child's academic life. When referring to "school ready," I do not mean that all academic concepts covered in this chapter are mastered before the first day of school. By using fun games and activities to teach these concepts, both preacademic and academic, we increase our children's motivation to participate in the learning process.

Some children require more opportunities to learn in a direct manner since they are not as likely as other children to learn through observation. When introducing the concepts that set up learning in specific areas such as mathematics and reading comprehension, it makes sense to infuse them into fun activities that capitalize on the strengths or sensory needs of your child; that way, they can generalize information. Thus, introducing or solidifying academic concepts through fun games and activities will help increase your child's opportunity to learn them.

Three-dimensional manipulation of objects and one's body as a way of learning is not the norm as our children progress up the grade levels. Within a few years of your child's entering school, most learning becomes pen-and-paper based (two dimensional) or computer based (one dimensional). But as we've seen, children with autism, Asperger's, or sensory disorders learn best in the three-dimensional world, by interacting in or with the environment, which is often a prerequisite to two- and one-dimensional learning. Learning in a three-dimensional way allows the brain and body to internalize complicated concepts to such a degree as to be able to understand the gestalt of the concept, thus allowing generalization of the information to other settings. Further, learning through experience, meaning active engagement in the learning process, has a much more powerful and residual imprint on our brain and body, thus establishing a stronger base for higher-level processing.

> **WHY** The *why* of this chapter is the same for each activity. Using three-dimensional learning as a way of imprinting preacademic and academic concepts in your child's repertoire of information will increase your child's opportunity for success in the classroom.

GAME ⑥³ Whose Turn Is It Anyway?

Indoor/Outdoor

- Either

Equipment

- Weighted ball (medicine ball, gym ball, therapy ball)

How (First Level)

- Create a series of simple questions. Gear the questions toward the participants' language level or interests. For example, "When you have the ball, say your name and your favorite animal," (substitute favorite TV show, favorite food, etc.).
- The person holding the ball is the speaker, singer, or actor.
- The participants will pass the ball among themselves.

How (Second Level)

- Move the activity up to the concept or category level, such as by saying, "Name something green," or "Name something that lives in the ocean."
- Suggestion for younger kids: have the person with the ball say an animal and the sound that goes with it.
- Suggestion for older kids: have the kids tell a story by having each successive participant add to the story as the ball is passed.

Purpose

- **Social interaction:** Turn taking, paying attention to others, and being the speaker in social situations all promote social interaction.
- **Attention skills:** Paying attention to others promotes one of the basic skills required to "get along" in a classroom environment.

- **Turn taking:** This activity uses sensory input to promote basic turn taking. The weighted ball serves as a visual reminder to the other children as to whose turn it is, as well as giving the child whose turn it is the cue to participate. This form of reminder is more effective than having an adult continually prompting children verbally, "Pay attention," or "It's your turn."

GAME (64) What's in My World?

Indoor/Outdoor

- Either, but preferably outdoor

Equipment

- For younger children: notebooks for storing pictures, pictures taken from the Internet
- For older children: a notepad

How

- Younger children prepare a notebook of pictures of people, animals, buildings, and so on that they expect to see during an activity (e.g., animals at the zoo).
- Bring the notebook to the activity, and have the child mark off the items he sees with a check mark or some other notation, such as a sticker or stamp.
- Have the child note a few things that he sees that were not included in the list before getting to the activity. The child might draw a picture of these things in the notebook.

- For older children, have them write a list of the things they expect to see and make checkmarks next to what they see.

Purpose

- **Observational skills:** This activity increases the child's awareness of his environment.
- **Visual projection:** Projecting what will be in the environment is a skill that helps decrease anxiety.
- **Memory:** This activity uses a visual support to aid children in remembering what they are looking for on a specific trip.
- **Language:** This activity is an effective way to attach language to visual information in the environment.

GAME (65) Back Writer

Indoor/Outdoor

- Indoor

Equipment

- Writing utensil
- Something to write on such as a piece of paper or small whiteboard

How (First Level)

- First write out the child's name on a piece of paper or whiteboard, and put it in front of the child.
- Rub the child's back as if erasing a whiteboard, using deep pressure.

- Draw lines with your finger to indicate that the top of the page is near the child's neck and the bottom of the page is near the child's lower back.
- Using your finger, write one of the letters from the child's name on his back. Press firmly when writing on the child's back.
- When it is time for a new letter, rub the child's back firmly with a flat hand.
- Have the child guess which one of the letters in his name you are writing on his back.
- When he gets good at guessing remove the visual prompt of his written name.
- Then have him guess the letter by writing the letter on paper or a whiteboard in front of him.
- You can expand to include other letters of the alphabet and then words.

How (Second Level)

- Have a peer write one of the letters of your child's name on your child's back; then have your child guess the letter being written. Children can take turns writing and guessing letters.

Note: We use this activity in our therapy clinic as part of our Social-Sense™ groups. It is so fun to watch kids who have a hard time with others touching them tolerate and even laugh while trying to determine which letter their friend is writing on their back. It also has the added benefit of helping the children in the group remember each other's name.

Purpose

- **Motor memory of letter formation:** Increasing motor memory for letter formation through touch decreases the reliance on the visual-motor system and increases success in writing.

- **Tactile sensitivities:** This activity mixes light touch and deep pressure, which will help the child tolerate the light touch if he experiences tactile defensiveness.
- **Social interaction:** Once your child starts to guess the letters correctly, you can include a peer, making it a fun learning game.

GAME (66) Go Fish

Indoor/Outdoor

- Indoor

Equipment

- The equipment needed is determined by your child. If she is at the color- and shape-matching level, use cards that have various colored shapes on one side.
- If she is at the letter-recognition stage, use cards with letters on one side. If you are working on numbers, you can use a standard deck of cards.
- If you are having a group of children play this game, you can purchase cards that display sets of animals. This can be a fun way for children of all levels to engage in this typical game.

How

- If playing with two players, deal eight cards each. If playing with three to six players, deal five cards each.
- Remaining cards are placed facedown in the draw pile.
- Choose a person (randomly) to go first.
- That person asks another player for a specific card type.

- If that player has any cards of the requested type, she must give them all to the player requesting: for example, give all of her 9s. If the player receiving the request has the requested card(s), then the player who made the request gets another turn.
- The requesting player may ask any player for any type of card, including the same type just requested.
- If the player asked has no relevant cards, he says, "Go fish." The player who made the request then draws the top card from the draw pile. If the requesting player happens to draw a card he requested, he shows it to the other players and gets another turn.
- However, if the requesting player draws a card that is *not* of the requested type, it is the next player's turn. The next player is the one who said, "Go fish."
- Each time a person collects four cards of the same type, she should immediately show the set to the other players.
- Winning occurs when a player has no cards left in his or her hand or when the draw pile runs out. Then the winner is the player who has the most sets of four.

Purpose

- **Components of executive function:** This activity involves organizing and assessing facts. Children must observe what is in their hand and deduce which card to request.
- **Working memory:** Children must remember what they are fishing for.
- **Modulation:** This game requires that the child suppress frustration (when not getting the desired card) and control reactions while waiting for the desired card.
- **Turn taking:** The game requires all participants to wait for their turn to participate.

- **Social communication:** Children are encouraged to engage in directly speaking to each other to keep the game going. Some children need adults to prompt them with verbal requests when they are first learning this game.

GAME 67 Seek 'n' Spell

Indoor/Outdoor

- Indoor

Equipment

- Small magnetic letters
- Pictures of things such as dog, cat, tree, and so forth
- Magnetic whiteboard
- Sandbox, or large plastic container of beans, rice, and so on

How (First Level)

- Cut out pictures of simple nouns, such as *cat, dog, pig, tree,* and *sun.* Post one picture at a time on the whiteboard.
- Hide the letters that correspond to the picture in a sandbox (or container of beans, rice, etc.) or throughout the room. (If you choose the room, make the letters fairly visible.)
- Have your child find the letters and then put them together to spell the word that corresponds to the picture.

Note: If this activity is too challenging for your child, write the corresponding word under the picture, and have your child search for the letters and match them to the word.

How (Second Level)

■ To make the activity more challenging, hide one or two additional letters in the sand so the child must discriminate which letters are needed to spell the word.

How (Third Level)

■ Increase the difficulty even more by having two pictures on the whiteboard and hiding the letters to spell both corresponding words.

Purpose

■ **Spelling:** This activity works on the spelling of simple words.

■ **Matching pictures to words:** It also promotes early reading skills.

■ **Tactile input:** It increases exposure to touch input as your child digs for letters in the sand.

■ **Visual input:** The activity involves scanning for hidden letters throughout the room (if you choose this option).

GAME (68) Letter Search

Indoor/Outdoor

■ Either

Equipment

■ Plastic letters or stiff cardboard letters (different colors): two sets of identical letters

How (First Level)

- Place the letters throughout the house in semivisible sites.
- Show your child a letter, and instruct her to go find the same letter.

How (Second Level)

- Show your child a word, and have her find all the letters that make up that word.

How (Third Level)

- Tell your child the word, and have her go find all the letters.

How (Fourth Level)

- Tell your child the word, and have her find the letters (as in the third level). Once she finds the correct letters, have her assemble them and write the word.

Purpose

- **Attention:** Tabletop activities can be very daunting for some children, especially those activities deemed as work. Infusing tabletop work in a game that requires motor engagement decreases perception of work and increases participation.
- **Letter recognition:** This activity promotes letter recognition by having your child identify the letters found.
- **Visual-perceptual skills:** The activity aids in visual discrimination by differentiating visual foreground information from background information.
- **Writing:** This activity offers a way to practice writing by providing your child with a visual prompt so the child can see the letters while writing the word.

GAME (69) Everyday Flash Cards

Indoor/Outdoor

- Indoor

Equipment

- Flash cards with pictures and word captions of everyday household items
- Timer

How

- Encourage your child to go around the house matching household items with the pictures in a given amount of time (e.g., 1 minute, 2 minutes).

Note: Because following auditory directions can be difficult for some children, you may have to hold the child's hand through the first round or so. Adjust for this by allowing a longer time period at first. As your child's skill increases, decrease the amount of time allotted.

Purpose

- **Word recognition and meaning:** Matching words to objects that your child sees in her everyday world promotes visual recognition of the word while attaching meaning to the word.
- **Visual skills:** This activity promotes visual scanning, since your child needs to scan quickly so she can beat the clock.
- **Visual-perceptual skills:** It encourages your child to visually discriminate foreground from background to visually perceive objects around her.

GAME ⑦⓪ Puzzling Obstacle Course

Indoor/Outdoor

- Either

Equipment

- Simple jigsaw puzzle (as complex as the child can accomplish)
- Bucket
- Cones, crawl tunnels, trampoline, hula hoops placed flat on the floor or held vertically—anything that makes a child think about how to move around, over, under an object

Note: You can make a simple puzzle. Download or take a picture of an item or a character your child likes, such as Thomas the Tank Engine; laminate it; and cut it into puzzle pieces. To simplify the puzzle for your child, you can also create the board that the pieces go on by using a white piece of posterboard cut to the size of the picture. Use Velcro pieces on the board, with matching Velcro on the puzzle pieces. You can further simplify the activity by drawing lines on the white poster board that define the puzzle pieces, providing your child with a visual cue of where to put each puzzle piece.

If you choose to make the puzzle, you can motivate your child to put it together by having the actual item in the picture available for him to play with after he finishes the activity. For example, have the Thomas the Tank Engine visible but out of reach and say, "When you put Thomas together, you get to play with him."

How

- Set up an obstacle course for the child.
- Have the child pick up a piece of the jigsaw puzzle (just one piece at a time) from a bucket and go through the obstacle course.
- At the end of the obstacle course, have a designated spot for the child to put the puzzle pieces together.

Note: If this is too challenging, hide the pieces in a sandbox and have your child assemble the pieces outside of the sandbox one at a time. To increase difficulty, hide the puzzle pieces throughout the obstacle course and have the child get one piece each time she goes through and place it in the puzzle.

Purpose

- **Inference:** This activity challenges the ability of the child to draw inferences, since the puzzle pieces are not all available when the child is assembling the puzzle. So the child must try to assemble the puzzle with limited information, or the parts-to-whole concept. Kids with autism spectrum disorder (ASD) often tend to focus on the smaller details.
- **Motor planning:** The motor planning system will be challenged by the child going through an obstacle course.
- **Visual-spatial skills:** Visual-spatial skills are challenged when the child collects and assembles the jigsaw puzzle. This activity also develops depth-perception skills and the concepts of directions and spatial relations.

GAME (71) Bigger, Better Letters

Indoor/Outdoor

- Outdoor

Equipment

- Chalk
- Spray bottle filled with water

How

- Draw different letters on the ground using the chalk.
- Have the child use the spray bottle to "clean up" the chalk letters by spraying in the same pattern used to create the letters.

Purpose

- **Letter recognition:** Any activity that immerses the child in forming letters, especially while moving, will increase letter recognition.
- **Motor understanding of letter formation:** By using gross motor movement to form letters, the body develops increased understanding of proper formation.

GAME (72) Letters, Letters Everywhere!

Indoor/Outdoor

- Indoor

Equipment

- Three 5-inch-by-8-inch index cards

How

- Choose a letter of the week. Write the chosen letter on the cards.
- Tape one of the cards to the back of the seat in your car (in front of where your child sits) and one on the refrigerator.
- The objective is to count how many times your child and you see the letter throughout the week.
- Look for the letter in store signs. For example, *S* in Starbucks, McDonald's, the stop sign, and so on.

Note: Another option is to cut the letter out of white paper and glue it onto a black piece of construction paper. This high contrast will make it visually easier for your child to match the letter to those in signs.

Purpose

- **Letter recognition:** This activity promotes letter recognition within the child's daily environment.
- **Word recognition:** Because your child is searching for the letter of the week within words he sees every day, this game offers increased opportunity to recognize familiar words.
- **Visual-perceptual skills:** Discriminating a letter from other letters in a word requires visual-perceptual skills, such as discrimination and foreground and background differentiation.
- **Visual scanning:** Your child must observe and visually scan the environment to search for the letter of the week.

Color Connection

. . . .

Indoor/Outdoor

- Indoor

Equipment

- Large sponge-tip applicator markers of different colors
- White poster board
- Black marker

How (First Level)

- Choose a color of the sponge tip applicator, and make large dots on the poster board that when connected create a shape.
- Tape the poster board to the wall, or clip it onto an easel.
- Have your child use a black marker to connect the large dots. If needed, take his hand and show him how to connect the colored dots.
- Talk him through the activity, "Let's draw a line from this dot to this dot . . . now to this dot. Look, you made a triangle!" The next time you do it, ask your child, "Where do we go next?"

How (Second Level)

- Using two different colors, make triangles and squares. For instance, make the triangles yellow and the squares red. Tell your child to connect all the yellows and then connect all the reds.
- You can use three or four different colors to create shapes on the poster board. Because the shapes are different colors, they can even overlap.
- Try numbering the colored dots to give order and to get your child accustomed to doing traditional dot-to-dots.

Purpose

- **Directionality concepts:** This activity works on directionality (e.g., down, across) while the child draws the lines. This is a prerequisite for writing.
- **Language concepts:** This is an excellent activity for infusing basic language concepts, such as *down*, *across*, *right*, *left*, *top*, and *bottom*.
- **Visual-motor coordination:** This activity promotes visual-motor coordination while using gross as well as fine motor skills because the writing surface is large.
- **Shoulder, arm, and wrist stability:** Because your child is working on a large vertical surface, he must use muscles at his shoulder, arm, and wrist to draw the connecting lines. This increases the stability of these joints.

GAME ⑦⑷ Paper Tracks

Indoor/Outdoor

- Indoor

Equipment

- Wooden craft sticks
- Glue
- Markers
- Stiff white paper
- A toy that has wheels and can be pushed along the floor that your child likes, such as a fire truck, Thomas the Tank Engine, Lightning McQueen, and so on

How (First Level)

- Tell your child, for example, that since Lightning needs race-tracks to drive on, he is going to make them.
- Put glue on a wooden craft stick and lay it lengthwise on the paper. Create two rows of sticks end to end going down the length of the paper, with enough room in between for Lightning to zoom on.
- Make at least three pieces of paper with stick rows on them. Then lay the sheets end to end to create a racetrack.
- Once you prepare one with your child, let him to do as much of the other sheets as he can.

How (Second Level)

- Create railroad tracks for Thomas, for example, by drawing lines lengthwise across the paper 2 inches a part and then lines connecting "long" lines.

Note: I work with a teacher who uses this activity as a way to get one of her preschool boys interested in using a marker or crayon to draw a line. Once he understood what he could create, the door was opened and the teacher used it to expand his use of writing utensils.

Purpose

- **Fine motor skills:** This fun activity has a purpose for those children not motivated to participate in fine motor tasks, especially using glue.
- **Directionality:** This is a great activity to work on directionality. Long lines are drawn *across* the paper, and short lines are drawn *down*.
- **Prewriting:** The first step of writing is to get your child engaged in using writing utensils to make lines. This activity is motivating because the child is making something that can be used with a highly motivating toy.

HOME ACTIVITIES

Activities carried out as part of daily living are quite full of opportunities for learning. The home setting is a rich setting to practice activities that promote fine and gross motor skills, develop cognitive capability, and provide innumerable chances to elicit language. Motor skills developed include bilateral integration when pouring liquid from a pitcher to a cup or buttoning a shirt. Core strength is increased with such activities as vacuuming or carrying the laundry basket. Many household activities help enhance cognitive skills; for example, setting the table requires sequencing and organization. Your home and daily life activities provide innumerable opportunities to teach language as well as open the door in a safe environment for your child to express himself verbally.

Because activities that we carry out in our homes encompass so much of our lives, it is natural to incorporate children into those activities by making them fun and even making games out of some of them. The home setting offers a safe environment since the people and places are familiar. Activities such as cooking and cleaning are perfect for practicing cognitive skills such as sequencing, using visual memory, applying early mathematical concepts, following auditory directions, as well as understanding the gestalt of a situation. One of the biggest benefits of household activities is that they by definition need to be practiced over and over again.

> **WHY** There is no doubt that by integrating your child into everyday household activities you will enhance his or her learning at every level. However, the main *why* behind creating or enhancing what we do every day in our homes is the functional independence that your child will gain, which will generalize to other activities of daily living that can be used throughout the child's life.

GAME ⑦⑤ Laundry . . . Fun

Indoor/Outdoor

- Indoor

Equipment

- Laundry

How

- The following suggestions can be done one at a time, or use a few simultaneously. Since laundry needs to be done so often, these suggestions can be stretched over a period of months.

- Sorting: Have the child sort the laundry (clean or dirty) in categories: light and dark; big and little; mine and yours; or shirts, pants, pajamas, and socks.
- Have fun with the textures, and have each of you try on "funny clothes" or attempt to wear each other's clothes.
- Ask, "Why does this not fit?" Encourage the child to try an adult's favorite shirt. "Who is bigger/smaller, taller/shorter?"
- Compare the sizes of adult's hands, feet, and length of legs with the child's.
- Ask child to follow one- or two-step directions with descriptive elements, such as "Pile up the blue towels, and put them in the closet," or "Find one of Daddy's long, white socks and your short pink sock."
- You can also pile clothes on the child (make sure not to cover the head) or put numerous socks or shirts on the child at a time.
- Have the child close her eyes, reach into the laundry basket, and grab an item. Encourage the child to describe or guess what she grabbed or who it belongs to.
- After the laundry is washed, the child can separate all the clothes according to who they belong to and can help with finding the matching socks.
- Let the child attempt to fold the clothes or roll the socks together. Motor the child through this part of the process at first so the child understands how to do it.
- Have a mirror or camera available so your child can see herself putting on different clothes.
- Put two different color or sizes of socks on, and ask, "Are these the same or different?"
- For your little ones, make the reward for participating in "laundry fun" a ride in the laundry basket.
- Encourage the child to sit carefully in the basket, and then push or pull her around on the floor.

Purpose

- **Muscle strength and coordination:** This activity requires muscle strength.
- **Language concepts:** This activity allows for opportunities to work on concepts such as *same, different, large,* and *small.*
- **Gross motor coordination:** Folding and carrying laundry requires gross motor coordination.
- **Fine motor coordination:** Rolling socks and buttoning while folding require fine motor skills.
- **Visual cognitive processing:** This activity involves the ability to recognize, match, and categorize information.
- **Sensory input:** Laundry games offer the opportunity to touch different textures, provide body-awareness activities as your child dresses up, and involve vestibular-proprioceptive skills, such as when carrying the laundry basket full of laundry.

GAME ⑦⑥ Sanitation Engineer

Indoor/Outdoor

- Indoor

Equipment

- House trash

How

- As with the laundry activity, the following suggestions can be done one at a time, or you can use a few simultaneously. Since trash night is once per week, the following suggestions can be stretched over a period of months.

- Encourage the child to go on a mystery hunt to find all the trash cans in the house, room by room.
- Have the child describe the room he is going to: "There is a shower in it," or "Mommy sleeps in there," or "We eat in there."
- After all the cans have been brought to one location, have the child put them in a line from tallest to smallest, fullest to empty, widest to most narrow, darkest to lightest in color, or heaviest to lightest.
- Pour the trash from the smallest can into the largest one, and see if it fills up.
- Encourage the child to guess which amount can fit into the other cans.
- Questions to ask include, "Is it half full or half empty?" "Is there anything that can be recycled?" and "Where does the trash go when it leaves the house?"
- After the trash cans have been emptied, have your child tell you where to return each one. Ask questions if the child does not provide enough information. Or "accidentally" put a trash can back in the wrong room and let the child correct you.
- Trash cans are also great musical instruments if they are clean. Grab a stick, hanger, shoe, or wooden spoon, and have the child "beat the drum."
- Encourage questions such as, "What sounds does a metal can versus a plastic can make?" "What does the can feel like? (e.g., soft or hard, smooth or rough, cold or warm)" "Can the cans stack up on each other? Fit inside one another?"

Purpose

- **Daily living skills:** Taking out the trash is an essential skill for health and cleanliness.

■ **Categorization:** Having the child separate the trash into different categories helps develop the child's ability to classify information.

GAME (77) Setting the Table

▪▪

Indoor/Outdoor

■ Indoor

Equipment

■ Large pieces of construction paper (the size of large place mats)
■ Black marker
■ Table items: plates, utensils, condiments, napkins

How

■ You and your child set a place by placing the construction paper on the table and putting down the common items for an everyday dinner (knife, fork, plate, etc.).

■ Use a black marker to help your child trace the items so each imprint is on the construction paper. Do one for every member of the family. Write the family member's name on the place mat. Make two extra place mats to be ready for friends.

■ Laminate the place mat by taking it to a copy shop or a similar establishment.

■ Using the visual cues on the place mats, your child can aid in setting the table.

■ Prompt your child by saying, "How many people are we having for dinner tonight?" If your child struggles to answer this question, help her count the number of people. Have the child match the number of people to the number of place mats set.

- The child puts the correct place mat in front of each family member's place.
- Tell the child what is being served for the meal, and ask the child what she thinks is necessary to put on the table: "What should we eat the soup with? A fork or spoon?" "Do we need a knife if we are having sandwiches?"
- Then have the child set the table.

Purpose

- **Daily living skills:** The visual cues provided by this activity give a visual map of the place settings, providing your child with a starting point for this everyday activity.
- **Visual-spatial skills:** Your child must understand the spatial properties of the object to match it to the place mat in much the same way as a noninterlocking puzzle.
- **Preacademic skills:** Matching, arranging (gestalt), and organizing are all preacademic skills.

GAME (78) Color Eating

Indoor/Outdoor

- Indoor

Equipment

- Construction paper of different colors
- Various foods based on the color chosen

How

- Once per week, encourage your child to choose a color of food for the week. Each meal should contain one food item of that color (three or four times that week will suffice).
- Go shopping and buy various foods in the chosen color. They can be foods your child normally eats, but try to use the game to buy "new foods" for your child.
- The object is color matching, so take the colored paper to the store with you and let your child walk through the store choosing matching foods.
- Another version of this game is to have your child choose different shapes and go shopping for foods that match the shape. You can also show your child how different foods can be cut to match the shape chosen.

Purpose

- **Color matching:** This activity encourages children to find matching colors in their environment.
- **Language:** It creates opportunities for increased vocabulary and language interaction as you and your child comb the grocery store seeking the various colored foods.
- **Nutrition:** Children who are picky eaters tend to eat only a few foods with a limited choice of color. In this activity, you focus on the color and not the food itself.

GAME ⑦⑨ Same Color Meal

Indoor/Outdoor

- Indoor

Equipment

- Foods of the same color
- Clothes of the same color as the food
- Stuffed animals of the same color as the food

How

- Make and eat a meal with everything the same color.
- Have your child go through the entire process with you—that is, go to the store (or your pantry) with you and pick out items.
- Use food coloring to make the milk change color, or encourage drinking something else that color.
- Have the child dress in clothes that are the same color, or have toys or stuffed animals the same color join your table.
- Encourage your child's imagination to name other things that are the same color or other words that start with the same sound (e.g., green: *go, grapes, good*).
- Try to incorporate as many things as possible that are the same color to promote awareness of items around the child and to expose the child to different foods.

Purpose

- **Daily living skills:** By learning how to prepare foods so they all have the same color, the child becomes aware of the foods he eats and how to prepare and manipulate them.
- **Increased palate:** This approach to food may be a good way to expand the repertoire of the picky eater, since such an eater may decrease sensitivity if involved in the process of the entire preparation regime.

WHY: Color Eating and Same Color Meal The two preceding activities are strategies to try for children who tend to be picky eaters or if you are just trying to expand your child's repertoire of food. Children with sensory processing disorder often have a limited repertoire of food, which can be related to sensory defensiveness. However, often after the sensory defensiveness has been "worked through," a child displays the same picky eating behaviors because it has become an engrained behavior. Making trying new foods part of a game will help introduce your child to new foods. This is one of many strategies, but it is definitely one of the more enjoyable ones!

GAME (80) Soapy Finds

Indoor/Outdoor

- Indoor

Equipment

- Bathroom with a bathtub
- Bubble bath
- Small (2-inch) floating bathtub toys

How

- Fill up bathtub with water and bubbles.
- "Hide" objects in the soap bubbles, and instruct the child to go look for them.
- Once the child finds an object, have him explain what it is, its color, and its shape.

Purpose

- **Communication:** Using the bathtub ritual (most kids like baths with bubbles), this activity is a way to make bath time into speech therapy time. You can elicit language by asking the child to identify the objects, make the noises associated with the objects, and so on.
- **Shape, color recognition:** By having the child identify shapes, colors, and objects, you promote communication and a more solid understanding of descriptive language.
- **Sensory:** Playing with water is a rich way to integrate various components of the touch sense.

GAME (81) Plan a Picnic

Indoor/Outdoor

- Either, but preferably outdoor

Equipment

- Masking tape
- Small pieces of paper (label-sized), or stickers used for postage return labels
- Blue or black marker
- Plastic bags that zip closed (quart-sized)
- Various finger-food items for your picnic—small items that can fit in a quart-sized bag are best, such as peanuts, apple slices, chips, crackers, grapes, and so on
- Larger bag or small cooler
- Paper plates and napkins
- Small blanket or old tablecloth
- Plastic cups and drinks

How

- When doing this activity for the first time, it is best that only two people go on the picnic: you and your child. Once the concept is learned, your child can invite others to the picnic (real and imaginary friends).
- First, start writing the food or items you will take on the picnic on the paper or the labels. Make sure to leave plenty of room on the labels to write the number of the said item.
- Now decide how many of each item you and your child will bring to the picnic. Prompt your child by saying, "Since there are two people—me and you—having a picnic, how many apple slices should we bring?" If he says one or two, prompt him to rethink his figure. "One—so you will eat one apple slice and they will be all gone. I will get none? What if you want two apple slices, and I want two apples slices? Let's count and see how many we should bring."
- Once the number is decided upon, write the number below the name of the food: "Apple slices, 4." You can encourage your child to write the names of the food and the numbers if she is able to, but remember the names and numbers have to be written clearly so she can read the numbers later.
- Use the label-sized pieces of paper or simply peel the labels off, and place them on various plastic bags.
- After you have made labels for three to five different foods and their numbers, take one bag at a time and help your child read the item and identify its number, such as "peanuts, 8." Then have the child count out the items and put them in the bag.
- Place all the bags in another large bag or a small cooler. Get your blanket and two plastic cups with your chosen drink.
- Head off to your destination: the backyard, the living room, or the park. Let your child set up the picnic, including putting

the foods on each of your plates and counting the number of food items for each of you.

- Alternative: If your child cannot identify words and numbers yet, use small pictures from the Internet or digital pictures of the foods and large dots to indicate the number of each food item. Tape the pictures and dots to each bag, and encourage your child to fill each bag with the correct number of each item.

Note: This game came about because I was working with a nine-year-old girl whose father wanted some ideas for activities that incorporated some of the learning concepts that were important to teach her but would allow him to feel like he was spending some "downtime" with his daughter. The idea was to have them work on an activity together that could fill a Saturday afternoon and that she would look forward to. This activity turned out to be a winner for both the dad and the daughter. They do it almost once a month, and it has gone from him doing a lot of the prompting, "Are you sure we don't need more crackers?" "Is one sandwich enough for two people?" to her questioning him and even remembering how many of a particular item he ate on the last picnic.

Purpose

- **Counting:** This activity encourages simple rote counting.
- **One-to-one correspondence:** It has the child match the visual number to the amounts.
- **Recognition of numbers and words:** This activity provides many opportunities to practice reading numbers as well as writing them.

GAME (82) Party Planner

....

Indoor/Outdoor

- Either

Equipment

- Poster board
- Marker
- Party materials: plastic plates, cups, utensils
- Depending upon how elaborate you want to make the party, you can add balloons, party streamers, horns, and so on

How

- Make a set of columns on the poster board with room at the top for labeling each column.
- Label each column based on what your child wants to have at the party, including food and entertainment (e.g., music, bouncy house). The leftmost column is for names of the other attendees, real and imagined.
- Your child's name is first. Below his name, list the names of the children whom he thinks he may want to invite to the party.
- Have your child "analyze" the other kids to see which children have similar likes as his, such as pizza or pirates. Then he can put a checkmark in the columns that correspond with each kid's likes.
- This is an opportunity for you to help your child understand that other children have different likes and dislikes and that he should invite people with common likes.
- After you have narrowed the list down (the first time you do this activity, I recommend limiting the list to three to four chil-

dren), have your child work with you to design invites (the Internet has some great premade invites). Make sure to encourage your child to sign his own name on the invite.

- Now make a list of the activities—only a few, you don't want this party experience to be too overwhelming for your child.
- Leading up to the party, role-play how your child will greet friends at the door, what he will tell friends and talk to them about, and how he will take turns and thank friends for coming to the party.

Note: It is important that you and your child talk about what strategies he will use if the party becomes overwhelming. For example, will there be a safe place in his home where he can go to take a "party break," or will there be gross motor activities that require *no* social interaction, which he can escape to if need be?

Purpose

- **Theory of mind:** To determine who fits this profile, your child must determine if another child's likes match the likes of the other children he is planning to invite.
- **Organization and planning skills:** This activity uses the motivator of a party to help your child learn how to plan an event and organize the materials needed for the event.
- **Emotional regulation:** Although emotional regulation is a goal in most of the activities in this book, the concept of having your child plan and then participate in a party is a way to help children who are anxious in social situations to prepare themselves and thus use emotional regulation strategies.

GAME (83) Sensory Cooking Activity

Indoor/Outdoor

- Indoor

Equipment

- Food preparation equipment: pots, pans, mixing bowls, food preparation utensils
- Sugar cookie dough (store bought or made from an easy recipe)
- Cookie cutters of geometric patterns
- Marshmallow crème, ripe banana, vanilla, blue food coloring
- 3-inch-by-6-inch note cards

How

- Create a note card for each step of the written directions. If your child is not at reading level, use pictures.
- Cut the sugar cookie dough using the cookie cutters, and bake according to the package or recipe instructions.
- In quart-sized bowl mix together a half cup marshmallow crème; 1 ripe banana, smashed; 1 teaspoon vanilla; and 2 drops blue food coloring. Have your child mix all the ingredients with his hands. Please be sure to have him wash his hands immediately prior to this part.
- If your child is tactilely defensive, he can wear thin plastic gloves.
- Matching pairs of similar geometric shapes, have the child spread the mixture on one cookie and place the other on top to make a sandwich.

Note: To further increase tactile input, create the sugar cookie dough from scratch and encourage your child to touch the butter, oil, and dry flour.

Purpose

■ **Tactile input:** Mixing a multitude of ingredients in a bowl provides multiple types of tactile input, including resistive, gooey, slimy, and sticky.

■ **Following directions:** This activity requires that the child follow sequential directions.

■ **Hand strengthening:** Mixing, rolling dough out with a rolling pin, and/or pounding out the cookie dough with the hands offers muscle resistance. Thus this is a strengthening exercise to the large muscles of the shoulder girdle and arms as well as the small muscles of the hand and fingers.

■ **Bilateral coordination:** Both hands are required to work together throughout this activity; for example, one hand must stabilize the bowl while the other hand squishes the banana and stirs the marshmallow-and-banana mixture.

Note: I've seen otherwise very picky eaters try new things because they were part of the process of making it. Also, the same child who refuses to participate in a craft project will work hard at decorating a cookie!

9

OUTDOOR ACTIVITIES

Since our children are developing nervous systems, we need to consider how the development of the nervous system has depended for millions of years on being outdoors. A developing nervous system desires to experience all the sensations that exist in the natural world of the whooshing wind, singing birds, and fragrant pines. It is crucial that some of the activities we engage our children in be conducted outdoors. No other stage or playground offers the nervous system such a dynamic array of input, sensory and cognitive.

The activities designed for this chapter need to be performed outdoors because the learning experience would be very difficult to duplicate indoors. With that said, I suggest moving any of the previously detailed games and activities in this book outside if you can. Since being outside enhances a child's sensory awareness, it increases the *learning experience* of most of the previous activities. There are ways in which the body, driven by the nervous system, processes information outdoors that cannot be replicated in an indoor environment, especially when it pertains to visual, auditory, and vestibular processing skills. Simple activities like throwing a ball become more dynamic simply from being outside, because of the varying types of visual information such as changes in depth dimension. Many other activities are more challenging to the nervous system when we are outdoors. For example, the simple act of walking requires increased motor planning because of the varying terrain of the outdoors.

Some experiences cannot be replicated indoors. For example, when a child hears the rustling of branches, his auditory system attends to the information and localizes and discriminates what the sound is instantaneously. His vestibular system working with his musculoskeletal system allows him to crane his neck, altering his head in a spatial plane while maintaining his balance. The small muscles of his eyes, which are controlled by his vestibular system, coordinate his eyes so they work together to locate the source of the rustling leaves and focus as a small bird emerges from a cacophony of chirping and squawking.

Note: Visual activities abound in this book, but the outdoors is by far the richest environment to "work out" the eyes. More and more children struggle with visual skills that impact their success in the classroom as well as on the playground. Younger children are spending more and more time in front of a pixilated screen. A 2003 Kaiser Family Foundation study reported that 68 percent of children under the age of two spend more than two hours per day in front of a media screen. It is imperative for our children's development that we balance the sedentary visually taxing input received from media screens with movement-based, visually stimulating, auditory-rich outdoor activities.

Outdoor (Visual) Library

Indoor/Outdoor

- Outdoor

Equipment

- Camera
- Photo paper

How

- Take pictures of animals, birds, trees, rocks, and so on. Be sure to take pictures of items separately.
- Print out the pictures, and spread them out.
- You (the adult) determine a scene, and the child groups together the objects that belong to that scene (e.g., lake, duck, boat).
- Alternatively, have the child group the pictures together by a category such as animals, trees and flowers, things that fly, and any category that you have enough pictures to make a group.
- As the child advances (and the library becomes large enough), have the child build collages based on a theme or scenario.
- Develop the library over time, and pull it out regularly.

Purpose

- **Categorization:** By using visual cues, this activity helps your child's brain to categorize past sensory experiences.
- **Reading comprehension:** This activity prompts your child to categorize and access information in the brain in a fashion similar to when the child listens to a story or reads a book.
- **Memory:** By prompting your child to link associated information together, the activity helps your child understand the gestalt of the experience.

- **Ocular-motor skills:** This activity exercises the muscles of the eyes by encouraging a range of visual movements, including wide motility, scanning, eye pursuits, and eye saccades.

> **WHY** One of the reported brain-processing differences of children with neurological difficulties, especially autism spectrum disorder (ASD) and Asperger's, is difficulty understanding the gestalt of a situation versus the details. This game helps your child understand the larger context, the gestalt, of a situation.

GAME ⑧⑤ Inside Out

Indoor/Outdoor

- Outdoor only

Equipment

- 8½-inch-by-11-inch paper and pen

How

- Draw a line down the middle of the paper, creating two columns. Label one column "Indoor" and the other column "Outdoor."
- In the "Indoor" column, name common indoor items and their touch properties: for example, *the blanket—soft, leather couch—smooth, drink in refrigerator—cold, water from faucet—wet, needle—prickly.*

- Now go outdoors and find matching tactile properties: for example, *lake—wet, rose thorn—prickly, dog—soft*.
- In the "Outdoor" column, write the outdoor item and sensation that corresponds to a similar indoor item and sensation.
- Try to do things like this whenever you go on vacation.

Note: I can tell when parents have played this game with their child during a trip. When I see them after the trip, my simple question, "Was the trip to Tahoe fun?" is not met with a quick yes or no, but with information about what they saw and felt.

Purpose

- **Tactile skills:** Linking common tactile properties to outdoor objects helps the child generalize the already learned sensory information. Also, this links visual and touch information together.
- **Visual skills:** This activity encourages a wide range of ocular motor skills due to being outside.
- **Language:** Showing your child how a descriptive definition of an object or experience used in daily life applies to the properties of objects outside the confines of the house expands the child's understanding of descriptive words.
- **Reading comprehension:** Having an expansive understanding of words and how they apply to many things increases your child's understanding of words in context.

WHY Although children can understand what a word means by reading or hearing about it, evidence shows that experiences increase a child's understanding of words, which has a later impact on reading comprehension as well as on writing.

GAME (86) Walks 'n' Talks

Indoor/Outdoor

- Outdoor

Equipment

- None—maybe some hiking boots
- Place to hike
- Camera (second level)
- Small notebook and writing instrument (second level)

How (First Level)

There are innumerable ways to make a hike interesting, especially as a means to elicit communication.

- Walk *behind*, *in front of*, or *next to* each other and talk about the prepositions: for example, "I am next to you." This is the best way—concrete and three-dimensional—for your child to understand these concepts.
- Pick up sticks along the way, and analyze the stick collection: for example, "Which one is longer (shorter, heavier, lighter, sharper, or smoother)?" For more advanced children, this can take the form of a question-and-answer game: for example, "Who has the longest stick?"
- Alternate fast-slow walking, and describe the rate of walking and any changes such as stopping, turning, or taking big or small steps.
- Use counting steps as a means to teach direction, and follow by saying things like, "two steps forward, four steps back." For children who have difficulty with directions—specifically children

who have receptive language or motor planning difficulties—you may have to motor them through it. Hold the child's hand while you walk her through the directions.

- Play the "look up and down" game. Ask, "What do you see?" For example, use the carrier phrase, "I see a something . . ." to start a conversation.

- To make the hike into a game, choose an object and see how many you can count. For example, ask, "How many pine trees do you see?"

- Play "follow the leader" as you walk around the neighborhood.

- Count the cars in the driveways. Choose and find a house or car of a certain color.

- Conduct the walk in the woods whenever possible. The sensory experiences and opportunity for expanded language opportunities are nearly infinite.

How (Second Level)

- To enhance recollection of various aspects of the experience, bring a camera and create a storybook of the hike. Every experiential story should include many pictures of your child with various backgrounds and objects, and the story should be in sequential order. Keep it short—no more than ten picture pages—and use simple words: for example, page one says, "On Friday, my mom and I went for a hike by the lake," and page two begins, "The first thing we saw . . ."

Purpose

- **Praxis (motor planning):** Although walking requires very little praxis and is done quite naturally, hiking in an unfamiliar environment or over a new terrain requires the brain and body to work together to navigate the novel environment.

- **Proprioceptive input:** Having your child hike up a hill provides a significant amount of proprioceptive input, as compared to walking on a level terrain that is familiar to your child's brain and body.
- **Communication/language:** Having your child learn to comment on her environment is a great conversation starter and is essential for the development of social language.
- **Language concepts:** This activity sets the stage for teaching expanded language, specifically questions about what is being observed and answers to questions.
- **Visual-spatial skills:** This activity promotes visual-spatial understanding of the environment by attending to similarities and differences in the properties of the things your child sees every day. It also links words with the observations.
- **Visual skills:** Again, being outside is the greatest "gym" for the eyes!

> **WHY** One of the best ways to begin a conversation with another person, especially someone who is not familiar to us, is to comment on the common surroundings or ask a question about the surroundings, such as "The sky is so clear today," or "Do you know if it will rain today?" Since so many children struggle with pragmatic language, it is important to provide activities that can be linked to expanded language and let them learn these skills in context.

GAME (87) Near 'n' Far

Indoor/Outdoor

- Outdoor

Equipment

- Four sticks: two flat sticks of wood of the same length used for mixing paint, a stick that is approximately 6 inches longer, one flat stick 9 to 12 inches longer
- Red paint

How (First Level)

- Paint the two flat sticks bright red on both sides. While painting the sticks, discuss how they are both the same size. Measure them so the child is convinced they are the same.
- Place the first stick in the ground. Then walk about 100 feet away, and place the second stick in the ground.
- Go back to the original stick and back up approximately 10 feet so that both sticks are in view.
- Point out that the stick that's farther away looks smaller even though it is not.

How (Second Level)

- Take the longer stick and place it at the farther away spot. Have your child go back to the original vantage point, place the longer stick in the ground, and run back to you.
- Point out to your child that the "near" stick (the shorter one) and the "faraway" stick (the longer one) look like they are the same size.

- Next place the sticks next to objects in different environments, such as on hikes or walking in the neighborhood, to get a sense of the perception of size of near and faraway objects.

Purpose

- **Visual-perceptual skills:** This activity promotes an understanding of how distance impacts the perception of size.
- **Visual skills:** Looking far and then near promotes visual scanning and eye motility, while focusing on the faraway stick encourages steady fixation.
- **Convergence and divergence:** For the eyes to take in the "near" stick, they must converge (move together) and then diverge (move apart from each other) to look in the distance.

WHY Activities that promote looking near and far at objects require depth perception, which relies on information from monocular vision (obtained through one eye) as well as binocular vision (both eyes working together—eye teaming). Incidentally, the eye muscles required for reading and that control convergence of the eyes (prerequisite binocular vision) are the opposing eye muscles that control for divergence (think biceps versus triceps), which allows the eyes to take in a pixilated screen or look in the distance (TV or computer). Thus, providing children with outdoor activities is even more crucial in a media-filled world.

Indoor/Outdoor

- Outdoor

Equipment

- Favorite toy characters such as Thomas the Tank Engine, or SpongeBob

How (First Level)

- Choose one of the characters, and explain that the character likes to be outdoors. For example, Thomas is always outdoors pulling cargo, SpongeBob goes to the beach, or Dora and Diego spend their entire time in the jungle.
- Prompt the child to go outdoors by saying that the character needs to go out because that is what makes the character happy and learn.

How (Second Level)

- Go for a walk and have the child name one thing that the character sees, smells, or hears. Once the child understands the different senses and can name one thing, then increase it to two, and so on. The idea is to use the character as a conduit for getting your child to attend to the sensory world around him or her.

Purpose

- **Outdoors:** For those children who are not motivated to explore the outdoors, this is an entryway into outdoor play.
- **Sensory awareness:** Using a character that your child relates to will serendipitously let him explore the outside environment. I have seen a child spend hours driving "Snow Thomas" around in

---

the snow because Thomas loves being outside! This same child would not go outside and "play" in the snow before Snow Thomas was introduced into the scenario.

- **Language:** The opportunities for vocabulary expansions, spatial concepts, comparisons, and asking simple cause-and-effect, "What if . . . ?"–type questions are abundant outdoors: for example, "What happens if the sun goes behind the clouds?"

> **WHY** Motivation is the key for expanding a child's world, and sometimes the greatest motivator is already in the child's hand!

GAME (89) My Secret Outdoor Path

Indoor/Outdoor

- Outdoor

Equipment

- Chalk or yellow rope (at least 10 feet of rope)
- Box with treat(s) or prize, chosen by the child
- Shoes (including an adult's shoes, sneakers, dress shoes)
- Electrical tape

How (First Level)

- Together with the child, you (the adult) help her construct a path, be it chalk or rope. If the child is capable of doing it herself, then let her draw the chalk line or lay the rope to make the path.

- Put the prize at the end of the path.
- Have the child walk on the chalk line as if on a tightrope—first in everyday shoes, then in less commonly used shoes, and then in an adult's shoes. Increase the difficulty by having the child wear different shoes (i.e., nonmatching) on each foot.
- Increase the difficulty further by zigzagging the line.

How (Second Level)

- Using the yellow rope, lay it throughout the backyard (on the ground): around a tree, over rocks, or over mounds (use strong tape, such as electrical tape, to secure the rope).
- Have the child attempt to walk the "tightrope."

Purpose

- **Ideation phase of praxis:** This activity reinforces all stages of praxis, including ideation (first stage of praxis) since the child aids in setting up the path.
- **Motor planning phase of praxis:** The child has to plan how her body is going to stay on the path when going around the tree or over the rocks.
- **Execution phase of praxis:** To complete the praxis stages, the child must execute the idea and plan by motorically following the path all the way to the chosen prize.
- **Visual tracking:** The child needs to visually follow the path while walking in order to stay on it.

WHY Most activities for children with difficulties are set up by an adult, and children are not part of the ideation or planning phases of the game. This activity allows the child to mentally and physically be involved throughout the entire activity.

GAME (90) Adventure Bag

Indoor/Outdoor

- Outdoor

Equipment

- Blunt-end tweezers
- Closed-end chopsticks, obtainable at many Asian restaurants as an option for children
- Large kitchen tongs
- Bag (Call it the adventure bag.)
- Paper and pen

How

- Young children: Use the tweezers, chopsticks, tongs, and bag. Have the child walk around filling the bag by using the appropriate tool based on the size of the item he chooses to place in the bag.
- Older children: If your child is at writing level, have him make a list of what he will search for and put in his bag. Then have your child search for the items outside and fill his bag with the listed items using the tool of choice.
- This would be a great activity to do with one friend. Working as a team, they can search for all the items on the list. One child should be responsible for holding the grabbing tools and list, while the other child holds the adventure bag.

Note: You may have to guide your child's list selection. Also, if your child struggles with writing, write the items for him as he dictates them. Or if he can, let him use the computer to generate the list, since the idea is to generate the ideas and have an outside purpose.

Purpose

- **Project planning:** This activity is designed to help children plan what they will search for, create a list, and then execute the plan.
- **Writing:** It motivates children to write, because the words have a purpose. This is very important for children who struggle with writing.
- **Social interaction:** This activity is a good "one friend"–type activity, which may be less stressful for your child than an indoor game or free time.

10

ADAPTING
BRAND-NAME GAMES

M ANY, MANY BRAND-NAME games offer opportunities to practice and further enhance many of the skills and concepts
learned through gross and fine motor play, sensory input, and
communication activities, as well as social sense development.

THE *WHY* OF THIS CHAPTER

It is well known that children with autism, Asperger's syndrome,
sensory processing disorder, or another neurological diagnosis
miss out on participating in many "typical" children's games. There
are many reasons children do not participate in these games: the
game is too sensory stimulating, the directions are not clear, the
motor components are too difficult, the language requirements
are too advanced, or the social component is overwhelming. The

reason I have included this chapter is to recommend some games that these children can access with success. The goal is to make them familiar with the idea of being successful at games so that they can expand their repertoire of games. Some of the games were chosen because of their simplicity or their ability to elicit language, facilitate motor control, increase sensory modulation in social situations, and at the same time be sufficiently motivating (read: *fun*) for the child to participate in long enough to absorb these benefits.

Also, many of these children demonstrate difficulty playing with some toys, due to difficulties with sensory processing, especially as related to motor planning skills. They cannot figure out how to manipulate many store-bought toys that fill our homes. The following games were chosen to provide a mix of opportunities for toy object manipulation as well as to expose children to typical reciprocal-type games that can be played with peers. Peers who may have higher-level skills are often willing to play games that are familiar to them, even when they have been slightly modified.

GAME (91) Whac-A-Mole

Indoor/Outdoor

- Indoor

Equipment

- Whac-A-Mole by Milton Bradley
- Three small plastic cups

How

- The objective of Whac-A-Mole is to hit your mole with a hammer when it makes a certain noise or lights up. There are four moles with different colored hats that come fused to the moles. Have your child choose to hit his or her favorite color.
- Play commences when you turn on the game. The game will begin to play music, and the moles will light up randomly. Have your child hit his or her mole with the provided plastic hammer when it lights up.
- As this game may provide too much visual information, auditory information, or both at one time for some children with autism, it can be adapted by placing three cups over the moles and teaching your child to hit his or her mole only when it lights up. Placing the cups on the moles' heads reduces the visual stimulation, since it reduces the number of lighting-up moles.
- You can make the game more interactive by taking a second cup off and joining your child in the game. Sit on the opposite side, hitting your mole when it lights up.

Purpose

- **Decreased frustration:** This teaches your child how to play a common game while decreasing frustration. Once the child gets accustomed to the game, you can involve peers.
- **Visual-motor control:** Responding to a visual cue with a motor action helps with visual-motor timing.
- **Attention:** The game increases attention skills, as the child must focus on the mole continuously.
- **Sensory filtering:** The activity requires the child to screen out auditory input to focus on hitting the mole when it is his or her turn.

Indoor/Outdoor

- Indoor

Equipment

- Hungry Hungry Hippos game (Hasbro)
- White 4-inch-by-6-inch note cards
- Blue, green, yellow, and pink markers
- M&Ms

How

- Draw a circle on each card with a color that matches one of the four hippos that come with the game.
- Make three cards for each color: one with one dot, one with two dots, and the third with three dots—*draw the dots inside the circles.*
- Start with two players (you and child); each player chooses a color.
- Stack an equal number of cards in a pile next to each participant.
- Each player (alternately) chooses a card.
- The player gets to hit the lever corresponding to the number of dots on the card.
- As the child becomes accustomed to the game, more people can join the game.
- To motivate counting, have each child count the number of marbles obtained; each participant gets the same number of M&Ms as the largest marble count.

Purpose

- **Cause and effect:** A simple action results in a hippo opening its mouth and gobbling up marbles. This is good for children with limited motor skills because the actions involved are simple and result in the desired effect.
- **Turn taking:** Drawing a card between turns uses a visual cue to instill turn taking, which decreases frustration. (This game is very chaotic when all participants "go" simultaneously.)
- **Counting:** The child counts the dots on the card to know how many times he can press the back of the hippo, which coordinates motor actions with numbers.
- **Social interaction:** Once a peer is brought into the game, it becomes social.
- **Simple rules and structure:** This adapted version decreases frustration through the addition of simple rules.

GAME ⑨③ Rainbow Rollers *or* Car Track

Indoor/Outdoor

- Indoor

Equipment

- Car Track (Melissa & Doug) or Rainbow Rollers (Alex)

How (First Level)

- When playing with a young child who demonstrates limited eye contact and expressive speech, place a car on the top of the track and point to it as it goes down the track.

- Do this several times until your child begins to watch the car go down the track.
- Now hold the car at the top of the track, and wait until your child looks at you or utters something. Then verbally acknowledge his request, and let the car go down the track.
- Then do it again. Your child will begin to understand that any attempt at communication—verbal or gestural and even eye contact, depending on the child's level—will elicit the outcome he wants.

How (Second Level)

- When playing with a young child who has some expressive speech and is learning how to request items in his or her environment, use this toy to teach your child how to ask for something. Hold the car, and when your child gestures for the car, ask him, "What do you want?"
- If he continues to gesture, prompt him by saying, "Car, you want the car."
- Now give him time to respond. He may start out by saying, "car," or something that sounds like it.
- Make sure to give him the car immediately, thus reinforcing his verbal request.

How (Third Level)

- This is a great toy to use to reinforce color concepts.
- Hold a different color car in each hand, and ask your child, "What color do you want?"
- Prompt a verbal answer by asking, "Red?" and extending the hand holding the red car. Then say, "Or blue?" and extend the hand holding the blue car.

- If your child reaches for one car, say, "You want the red car," and give it to him.
- The next time, slightly pull the car back and wait. This should get him to say the color of the car he wants.

Note: This is one of those toys that can change how you interact with a child. I have used this toy many times as a way of entering a child's world. I remember a mom and I working together to try to get her "little guy" to look at her. She really wanted that and tried so many different ways to get him to look at her. I brought out the racecar track, and he was fascinated by it. His mom started to hesitate before letting the car go down the track, and he looked at her as if to say, "Let it go, Mommy." She let the car go and hugged him, "Yes, yes, see the car go." He felt her enthusiasm, and in a short time they were playing a reciprocal game of cars.

Purpose

- **Joint attention and eye contact:** This activity involves eliciting joint attention by waiting and having the child indicate that he wants you to let the car go.
- **Expressive language:** Language concepts are best learned in the context of an activity, eliciting language in context.
- **Color recognition:** By teaching colors in the context of something motivating, you reinforce color concepts.
- **Visual-perceptual skills:** Watching the cars move along the track promotes saccadic movement of the eyes for smooth tracking.
- **Cause and effect:** The simple motor act of releasing the car produces the effect of the car rolling down the track.

GAME ⑭ Water Hot Potato

Indoor/Outdoor

- Outdoor

Equipment

- Hot Potato Splash (Fundex)
- Place to swim

Note: Children should always be supervised in a pool. If your child does not know how to swim, a life jacket is recommended.

How

- Played in the traditional fashion of Hot Potato, the players pass the potato around.
- The music plays (from the potato); the person holding the potato when the music stops is "It."
- The person who is "It" must do something, such as make a silly face, tell everyone his or her favorite color, or describe something around the pool or lake (e.g., tree, bird, etc.).
- This can be done in a backyard without water. However, the nice thing about the potato is that it floats. So if your child misses it, the potato does not actually fall.

Purpose

- **Social interaction:** This game promotes social interaction without much complication.
- **Motor planning:** Since the object of the game is to not be the one who is holding the potato, children learn to pass it along to the next person as quickly as possible, which requires motor coordination.

- **Auditory attention:** Your child must discriminate between the music of the potato, children laughing, and other auditory input in the environment.
- **Proprioceptive input:** Once your child becomes accustomed to water, it provides a proprioceptive blanket around the body, giving a sense of increased security. Thus the pool can be a great playground for promoting play.

GAME ⑨⑤ Bunny Hop

Indoor/Outdoor

- Indoor

Equipment

- Bunny Hop game (Educational Insights)

How

- Start the game with all of the bunnies in the patch.
- Everyone chooses a farmer, each with a different colored hat.
- Take turns rolling the dice; the roller pushes down a bunny of a matching color that is displayed by the die.
- The player pushes down on the farmer they chose, which will cause a bunny to pop up (not all of the bunnies pop up together).
- If the bunny they push down pops up, that player gets to keep it. Otherwise, the player needs to remember which farmer caused which bunnies to pop up.

Purpose

■ **Visual memory:** The child must remember which bunnies pop up when a particular farmer is pushed.

■ **Turn taking:** This game is fun and simple enough that many children will be able to wait for their turn. Also, children are motivated to attend while the other participants take their turn to see which bunnies jump.

■ **Executive function:** Since the child has to use working memory and planning, he must use components of executive function.

GAME ⑯ Hi Ho! Cherry-O

Indoor/Outdoor

■ Indoor

Equipment

■ Hi Ho! Cherry-O game (Hasbro)

How

■ Ask the child if she knows the rules. If so, have the child explain them. If not, explain the rules.

■ First have the child pick a tree and place all the cherries on the tree.

■ Then have the child spin. If the spinner lands on a number, that's the number of cherries the child takes off the tree and puts into her bucket. If it lands on a dog, she takes two cherries from her bucket and places them back on the tree. If it lands on the bird, she takes one cherry from her bucket and places it back on the tree. If it lands on the bucket of cherries, all her cherries are dumped back on the tree.

- When you don't have any more cherries on the tree, you win.
- Throughout the game, ask the children questions such as, "What number do you want to land on?"

Note: This games requires that a child exhibit basic fine motor skills (e.g., finger isolation) as well as rote counting skills.

Purpose

- **Language concepts:** Use of pronouns, such as in "*your* turn, *my* turn," as well as prepositions, such as in "Cherries are *under* the tree," "I landed *on* the dog," "We dumped the cherries *out* of the bucket."
- **Language expansion:** You can use this game to elicit discussion with "What if . . . ?" questions such as, "What happens if I land on number 3?"
- **Social rules:** This activity works on turn taking.
- **Math concepts:** It includes counting and doing one-to-one correspondence.

GAME (97) Crocodile Dentist

Indoor/Outdoor

- Indoor

Equipment

- Crocodile Dentist (Winning Moves)

How

- Each child takes a turn being the dentist. At each turn, the dentist pushes down a tooth he or she is "fixing."
- The crocodile bites down when a dentist hits a bad tooth, and that dentist (player) is out of the game.

Note: If your child seems afraid, let him or her hold the alligator while the other children push down a tooth. Or encourage him or her to push down the tooth with a wooden craft stick or a toothbrush to become acclimated to the idea that he or she will not be injured.

This is one of the all-time favorites with the occupational therapists and speech therapists at our clinic because it is simple. Also, kids from preschool up to fifth grade like it. It is fun to see how children who normally have a hard time engaging with others will start watching as one of the children slowly pushes down a tooth. You can see the other kids' shoulders pull up and their eyes get big, waiting to see if the crocodile's mouth is going to snap shut. It is a great way to start and end a group play or therapy time.

Purpose

- **Socialization:** This fun game allows children to participate in a group setting and promotes simple turn taking.
- **Sensory modulation:** This activity promotes learning to tolerate or modulate to inconsistent reinforcement.
- **Fine motor skills:** Pushing one of the teeth down at a time, the child practices isolated finger movements by extending her index finger and keeping the other fingers flexed.
- **Socialization:** The child must practice turn taking.

GAME (98) Honey Bee Tree

. . . . .

Indoor/Outdoor

- Indoor

Equipment

- Honey Bee Tree game (International Playthings)

How

- Each player chooses a flower tray; it is recommended that you put a card with each player's name in front of his or her tray. The game allows two to four players.
- Each player takes turns by pulling leaves out of the honey tree.
- The goal is to not have the bees fall onto your tray, which will occur if the wrong leaf is pulled or if the tree is shaken too much.
- The winner is the player with the least amount of bees in his or her flower tray after all the leaves have been removed or all the bees have fallen.
- Increase difficulty by having all the players lie on their belly with a pillow under their chest. This increases the physical control needed to not shake the tree.

Purpose

- **Proprioceptive/tactile input:** To exhibit the motor control necessary for this game, your child must learn to grade the pressure used as well as time of his or her movement.
- **Fine motor:** The removal of the leaves is going to require a well-controlled pincer grasp.

- **Motor control:** The players need to carefully remove the leaves without shaking the tree in case the bees fall. Extracting the leaves in a steady manner requires fine motor control.
- **Cause and effect:** Children learn that the removal of the leaves leads to the bees falling.

GAME (99) Don't Spill the Beans

Indoor/Outdoor

- Indoor

Equipment

- Don't Spill the Beans game (Hasbro)

How

- This is a game for two or more players. At first, start with an adult and the child, depending on the child's level.
- Each player gets a pile of beans.
- The players take turns placing the beans inside the plastic pot. The idea is to place the beans in the pot without tipping it over.
- At some point a player's bean will cause the pot to spill over. All the spilled beans are added to the pile of the player who tipped the pot.
- The winner is the first player with no beans left in the tray.

Purpose

- **Social interaction:** This game requires turn taking and non-threatening interaction.

- **Upper-extremity strength:** This actvity requires using upper-extremity strength to stabilize the arm so the beans can be gently placed in the pot.
- **Fine motor skills:** A pincer grasp is used to place the beans into the pot without tipping it over.

GAME (100) Cranium Cariboo

Indoor/Outdoor

- Indoor

Equipment

- Cranium Cariboo game (Hasbro)

How

- Use the beginner version (there is an advanced version as well).
- You (the adult) choose the type of card to use in the game (choices: letters, numbers, colors, or shapes). These will be the cards drawn throughout the game.
- Prepare to play the game by following the directions that come with the game. Place the card facedown, put the balls in their places (shake the game a bit to randomize where the balls end up), and make sure the key is available.
- The directions are straightforward and simple: Each player chooses a card and attempts to match his or her card to one of the "magic doors." If a match is found, the player inserts the key to see if he or she finds a treasure ball. If yes, the player places the ball in the tumbling tidepool on the side of the game. If not, the player has to wait until the next time to see if he or she gets a ball.

- The next player chooses a card and repeats the process.
- The last player to find a ball gets the treasure.

Note: A good strategy to encourage turn taking in this game is to establish a rule that whoever has the key in his or her hand draws the card. You (the adult) then verbally prompt the children to pass the key to the next player and say, "Whose turn is it to have the key? Yes, Jake's turn. Jake has the key; that means he draws a card." If you do this in the beginning, children will start to pass the key without prompting.

I was playing this game with two preschool boys, and I had to prompt only a few times before one started handing his key to the other boy after his turn, saying, "Here's the key—your turn." I loved the exchange of both the physical object and the language! The great thing about this game is that children do not get the sense that they are playing against each other but rather with each other to open the treasure. That kind of joint attention is exciting to watch!

Purpose

- **Preacademic skills:** This game familiarizes your child with shapes, colors, numbers, and letters.
- **Turn taking:** As with most board games, this game requires each participant to wait for his or her turn to see if he or she finds a treasure ball.

GAME (101) Don't Break the Ice

Indoor/Outdoor

- Indoor

Equipment

- Don't Break the Ice game (Hasbro)

How

- Set up the game by inserting the cubes into the base ice rink.
- Each player takes a turn and taps one ice cube at a time with his or her mallet. As more ice cubes are knocked out, multiple cubes will fall beneath the rink at the same time.
- The winner is the player who does not cause the bear to fall in the broken ice.

Purpose

- **Social interaction:** This game requires turn taking and non-threatening interaction.
- **Upper-extremity strength:** This activity requires using upper-extremity strength to stabilize the arm so as to not break the ice.
- **Fine motor skills:** Lateral pinch and palmar grasp are needed to hold the mallet.
- **Proprioceptive input:** The child needs to grade the amount of force needed to hold the mallet as well as to tap the ice cubes (lightly or firmly).

GLOSSARY OF
COMMON TERMS

Academic/preacademic skills: Conceptual skills, such as letter and word understanding, as well as understanding of numbers and math concepts. Also, requires the ability to integrate previously learned facts with newly presented information.

Asperger's (also called Asperger syndrome, Asperger's disorder): An autism spectrum disorder (ASD), named after Austrian pediatrician Hans Asperger. It is characterized by impairment in social abilities; restricted, stereotyped patterns of behavior and interests; as well as normal cognition. Children with Asperger's typically do not display delays in language; however, they do struggle with pragmatic language.

Attention deficit/hyperactivity disorder (ADHD): A neurobehavioral development disorder that affects an estimated 1 in 20 children in the United States. It is twice as common in boys as in girls, and it is characterized by consistent inattention and impulsivity. Attention deficit disorder (ADD) is without the hyperactivity component.

Auditory discrimination: The ability to recognize small differences in sounds (e.g., "ba" and "pa," or the class bell from a fire drill). It also allows us to locate sound in a large space.

Auditory (hearing): The hearing sense, which allows one to locate, capture, and discriminate sounds.

Autism: A developmental disability that is marked by impairments in normal communication, social interaction, and behavior and usually manifests before the age of two or three. It is estimated that approximately 1 in 150 children are affected with an autism spectrum disorder (ASD), with boys four times more likely to be affected than girls. Reports have shown that early detection and intervention are paramount to limiting the disabling impacts of autism. Some of the behavioral characteristics of autism are:

- Impaired development in social interaction and communication, and a markedly restricted repertoire of activities and interests
- Absence or delay of speech and language, although specific thinking capabilities may be present
- Restricted, repetitive, and stereotyped patterns of behavior, interests, and activities
- Marked sensory processing difficulties, with one or many of the sensory systems impacted: visual, hearing, touch, vestibular (balance and motion), proprioceptive (body sense)

Bilateral coordination: The use of both sides of the body, both hands, both feet, as well as the head integrating with the core of the body. It relies on integrating information from the two sides of the body, which is *bilateral integration*.

Communication: The exchange of thoughts and information through body language, speech, or writing.

Crossing the midline: This refers to the ability to cross over the midline or middle of the body, easily and smoothly—for example, reaching across the body with the right hand to pick up a cup on the left side of body, or moving the eyes smoothly across a page, left to right, without moving head. This is a prerequisite for many sensorimotor and academic skills.

Dyspraxia: Refers to a disorganized or impaired ability to think of, initiate or plan, and carry out sensory and motor tasks.

Expressive language: Using tone of voice, gestures, words, and rate of speech; the language used to convey thoughts, feelings, or events.

Eye-hand coordination skills: The ability to coordinate the eyes to hand movement, allowing a person to copy, write, put together a puzzle, and cut accurately.

Eye skills: Eye skills refer to the ocular-motor skills of the eyes that require muscle, strength, coordination, and timing as with any other motor skills. The vestibular system controls the small muscles of the eyes. This is why occupational therapists will always look at the vestibular system's role if there are visual difficulties. It is important to note that a child may have twenty-twenty vision and still have visual skill deficits. Difficulties with eye skills impact academic behavior as well as physical coordination skills. Eye skills include:

- Saccades: Quick eye movements used for scanning
- Pursuits: Smooth tracking movements used to follow moving targets or to track a fixed target while the body is in motion
- Fixation: Ability of the eyes to keep focused on a nonmoving target
- Mobility: Ability of eyes to move in full range of motion
- Motility: Ability of the eyes to move
- Eye teaming: Ability of the eyes to converge and work together; allows for binocular vision; critical for reading
- Convergence: The movement of the eyes toward one another
- Divergence: The movement of the eyes away from each other, which the eyes must do when looking in the distance

Fine motor skills: The basic skills performed by the hand and fingers. They include gripping, pinching, pincer grasp (thumb to index finger to pick up small objects), thumb and finger opposition, and in-hand manipulation skills. Fine motor skills allow for functional skills such as buttoning, tying shoes, turning a doorknob, holding a pencil correctly, as well as using eating utensils.

Gustatory (taste): The tasting sense; it is one of two "chemical" senses.

In-hand manipulation skills: The skills developed through separation of the two sides of the hand that allow for a balance between skills and power. It is essential for the development of more refined fine motor skills.

Joint attention: An early social skill that allows people to share experiences of observing an object or event by following gaze or pointing gestures. It is the foundation for social development, language acquisition, and cognitive development.

Language: A set of symbols used by people to communicate. They can be written, spoken, or gestures (sign language).

Olfactory (smell): The smelling sense; it is one of the two "chemical" senses. It registers and categorizes information about the odors encountered by sensing the chemicals in the air.

Position in space: The ability to relate to objects in the environment as well as one's own body in terms of orientation and organization—for example, in front, behind, backward, and so on.

Pragmatic (social language): Includes rules, written and understood, concerning how people interact in social situations. Involves three communications skills:

- Using components of reciprocal language or relating a story, including staying on topic, taking turns in a conversation, and using verbal and nonverbal signals
- Ability to use language for different purposes
- Modifying language based on who you are communicating with (e.g., baby or adults, inside or outside, familiar person or stranger)

Praxis: Often referred to as motor planning, the ability of the brain to plan and carry out an action, motor or language. The steps of praxis are ideation, motor planning, and execution. We use more praxis when an action is unfamiliar to us or we are doing a familiar action in a new environment.

Proprioception (body position): Body awareness; the "left hand knows what your right hand is doing" sense. It communicates where all of the body parts are relative to the others and how they are moving in relation to each other.

Receptive language: The ability to understand what is heard and perceived from others' gestures and facial expressions. Before children can communicate their own thoughts and desires, they must first learn to connect meaning to objects and actions.

Sensory integration: The neurological process by which information from the body and the environment is taken in, analyzed, and categorized in the brain so meaning can be attached to it. The basic senses integrate in such a way as to give an immediate and complete picture of one's self and the world around him or her. For example, the visual system working together with the vestibular and proprioceptive systems allow for visual motor coordination, which lets one respond to a ball moving toward that person, extend the hands, and catch it.

Sensory modulation: The ability to receive sensory information, "monitor" the input, and then adjust accordingly. Sensory modulation disorder has three categories:

- Overreactive: Explosive, disruptive, and avoidant behavior
- Underreactive: Distracted and withdrawn
- Sensory seeking: Distracting behavior (fidgeters and crashers)

Tactile sense: The sense of touch that has two components:

- Discriminative: The ability to discriminate valuable information about the properties of what is being touched
- Defensive: Stimulated by light touch and often overactive in autistic children

Theory of mind: The term used to describe a set of mental processes that are used to plan, organize, strategize, and attend to and remember details. Impairments in executive function impact a child's ability to examine ideas, make plans, complete work in a timely manner, or ask for help as well as more information when needed.

Vestibular (movement-balance): The three-dimensional "you are here" marker allowing one to understand where the body is in relation to the ground.

Visual-motor integration: The ability to take images from a vertical to a horizontal plane, which are foundational for visual-motor skills.

Visual (seeing): The seeing sense, which provides one with information about the color, shape, and distance of objects from one another, as well as movement of objects and people.

Visual-motor skills: The ability to coordinate visual information with the movement of the body.

Visual-perceptual skills: The brain's ability to take in the visual information from the eyes, integrate it with information from the other senses, and make use of it. Visual-perceptual skills are broken down as follows:

- Visual discrimination: The ability to discriminate visual likeness and difference, figure-ground from foreground; visual closure (fill in visual information).
- Visual memory: The ability to visually recall past information.
- Visualization: The ability to take the visual information that you already know and use it to project a new visual scenario into the future.

BIBLIOGRAPHY

Ayres, A. J. (1979) *Sensory Integration and the Child*, Los Angeles: Western Psychological Services.

Ayres, A. J. (1972) *Sensory Integration & Learning Disorders*, Los Angeles: Western Psychological Services.

Baldi, H., Detmers, D. (2000) *Embracing Play: Teaching Your Child with Autism* (video), Woodbine House.

Baldi, H., Detmers, D. (2006) *Passport to Friendship* (video), Woodbine House.

Baron-Cohen, S. (2003) *The Essential Difference*, New York: Basic Books.

Baron-Cohen, S. (1995) *Mindblindness: An Essay on Autism and Theory of Mind*, Cambridge, MA; MIT Press.

Bauman, M., M.D., and Kemper, T., M.D. (2005) *The Neurobiology of Autism*, Baltimore, MD: Johns Hopkins University Press.

Biel, L., and Peske, N. (2005) *Raising a Sensory Smart Child*, New York: Penguin Books.

Dawson, G., Ph.D. (2005) *Face Processing in Individuals with Autism* (online), Medscape.

Delaney, T. (2008) *The Sensory Processing Disorder Answer Book*, Naperville, IL: Sourcebooks, Inc.

Dennison, P. E. and G. E. (1989) *Brain Gym. Teacher's Edition*, Ventura, CA: Educational.

Frick, S., and Hacker, C. (2000) *Listening with the Whole Body*, Madison, WI: Vital Links.

Goleman, D. (1995) *Emotional Intelligence*, 1st edition, New York: Bantam Books.

Goleman, D. (2006) *Emotional Intelligence*, 10th anniversary edition, New York: Bantam Books.

Goleman, D. (2007) *Social Intelligence*, New York: Random House.

Grandin, T. (1995) *Thinking in Pictures and Other Reports from My Life with Autism*, New York: Doubleday.

Greenspan, S., and Wieder, S. (1998) *Child with Special Needs: Encouraging Intellectual & Emotional Growth*, Reading, MA: Addison-Wesley.

Hannaford, C. (1995) *Smart Moves: Why Learning Is Not All in Your Head*, Arlington, VA: Great Ocean.

Healy, J. (1990) *Endangered Minds: Why Children Don't Think & What You Can Do About It*, New York: Touchstone.

Heller, S. (1997) *Vital Touch: How Intimate Contact with Baby Leads to Happier, Healthier Development*. New York: Owl Books.

Hillier, C., O.D., and Kawar, M. (2005) *From Eyesight to Insight: Visual/Vestibular Assessment and Treatment*, San Diego: M Kawar & Associates.

Hirsh-Pasek, K., Ph.D., and Golinkoff, M., Ph.D. (2003) *Einstein Never Used Flashcards*, Emmaus, PA: Rodale.

Howard, P. (2000) *The Owner's Manual for the Brain, Everyday Applications from Mind-Brain Research*, Atlanta, GA: Bard Press.

Koegel, L., Ph.D., and LaZebnik, C. (2004) *Overcoming Autism,* New York: Penguin.

Lawton-Shirley, N., and Oetter, P., *Sensory Integration & Beyond: Power Tools for Treating Children,* Seminar 2005.

Leaf, R., and McEachin, J. (1999) *A Work in Progress,* New York: DRL Books.

Liddle, T., and Yorke, L. (2004) *Why Motor Skills Matter,* New York: McGraw-Hill.

Mailloux, Z. (2007) "Play and the Sensory Integrative Approach," in Parham, L.D., and Fazio, L., *Play in Occupational Therapy for Children,* Boston: Mosby.

May-Benson, T.Sc.D. (2007) "A Theoretical Model of Ideation in Praxis," in Roley, S., Banche, E., and Schaaf, R., *Understanding the Nature of Sensory Integration with Diverse Populations,* Austin, TX: Pro-Ed.

Miller, L. J. (2006) *Sensational Kids—Hope and Help for Children with Sensory Processing Disorder (SPD),* New York: Perigee Books.

Ozonoff, S., Ph.D., Dawson, G., Ph.D., and McPartland, J., Ph.D. (2002) *A Parent's Guide to Asperger Syndrome & High Functioning Autism,* New York: Guilford.

Pinker, S. (1994) *Language Instinct: How the Mind Creates Language,* New York: William Morrow.

Rahmann, H. (1992) *Neurobiological Basis of Memory & Behavior,* New York: Springer-Verlag Technical.

Ratey, J. (2001) *User's Guide to the Brain,* New York: Vintage Books.

Remick, Dr. K. (2000) *Eyes on Track,* Folsom, CA: JF Publishing.

Schetter, P. (2007) *Best Practice Strategies and Interventions for Autism Spectrum Disorders,* UC Davis (Class).

Schetter, P. (2004) *Learning the R.O.P.E.S. for Improved Executive Function,* Galt, CA: Autism & Behavior Associates.

Squire, L., and Kandel, E. (1999). *Memory: From Mind to Molecules*, New York: Scientific American Library.

Wilbarger, P., and Wilbarger, J. (1991) *Sensory Defensiveness in Children Ages 2–12: Intervention Guide for Parents & Other Caretakers*, Santa Barbara, CA: Avanti Educational Programs.

Wynsberghe, D., and Noback, C. (1995) *Human Anatomy & Physiology*, 3rd ed., New York: McGraw-Hill.

INDEX